Betty Crocker's Cookie Book

Photography Director: Remo Cosentino
Illustrations: Ray Skibinski

 **Golden Press • New York**
Western Publishing Company, Inc.
Racine, Wisconsin

Seventh Printing, 1983
Copyright © 1980, 1963 by General Mills, Inc., Minneapolis, Minnesota.
All rights reserved. Produced in the U.S.A.
Library of Congress Catalog Card Number: 80-67072
Golden® and Golden Press® are trademarks of Western Publishing Company, Inc.
ISBN 0-307-09930-X

When you want a homemade cookie, nothing else will do. And that's as it should be. Because cookies add the right touch to a picnic or a banquet, to a midnight snack or a holiday dinner. To any occasion, in fact. Cookies are always just right.

But what cookies shall you choose? Are you planning a celebration? Grace your table with colorful cookies, like Fancy Bonbons, or delicate ones, like French Lace Crisps. Are there lunch-toters in the house? Think about baking hearty cookies, like Mixed Nut Squares. If you like anything—just as long as it's chocolate—choose Chocolate-Applesauce Bars or Caramelitas or Chocolate Crinkles.

There are so many other exciting flavors and kinds of cookies, too—from old-fashioned favorites, like Butterscotch Brownies and Gingersnaps, to welcome newcomers, like Granola Sunflower Nut Bars and more than a dozen other recipes that count on granola. You'll also find an extensive collection of cookies you can bake with whole wheat flour. (One's a recipe for Chocolate Chip Cookies.)

What if you're puzzling over which cookies will delight every guest at a children's birthday party or which cookies can be put together in a hurry or which cookies to bake for Christmas this year? Look for the lists of children's favorite cookies, cookies that are quick and easy to bake and cookies for Christmastime. They'll help you solve these dilemmas.

The chapters are organized by cookie-making techniques, so that if you feel like using your cookie press today, you can quickly find all the cookie-press recipes in one place. And that goes for cookies you bake in a pan and then cut into squares or bars, cookies you cut from rolled-out dough, cookies you drop from a spoon, cookies you mold and shape with your hands, refrigerator cookies and fried cookies. (You've never tried a fried cookie? See pages 91-92.)

And last, the very first chapter—All About Cookies. It's for you, whether you are a novice cookie baker or know your way around a rolling pin. Here are three pages crammed with hints you'll be glad you have at hand every time you bake cookies—be they filled or frosted, star-shaped or square, for a party or just for being good to yourself.

The Betty Crocker Editors

Contents

All About Cookies

How to Bake Cookies

- Read the recipe carefully before you start.
- Assemble utensils and ingredients on a tray for more convenient cleanup.
- Follow recipe exactly; measure accurately.
- Make all cookies in the batch the same size to ensure uniform baking.
- Use shiny cookie sheets at least 2 inches narrower and shorter than your oven so the heat will circulate around them.
- Grease cookie sheets only if recipe calls for it.
- Always place dough on a cool cookie sheet; dough spreads on a hot one. It will save time to work with more than one cookie sheet—you can fill a cool one while another is in the oven.
- Bake 1 cookie sheet at a time; use center rack.
- Check at the end of minimum recommended baking time. A minute can make a difference.

Tips for bar cookies: Use the exact pan size! Spread dough evenly to sides of pan.

Tips for rolled cookies. Rub flour into rolling pin cover and board cover for easiest handling. Roll lightly and evenly. Dip cutter in flour before cutting, and cut cookies close together to avoid re-rolls. Lift cutout cookies with spatula.

Tips for drop cookies: Spoon with a tableware teaspoon; push onto cookie sheet with a second spoon.

Tips for molded cookies: Take your time, make the cookies uniform and be sure the cookie sheet has cooled between bakings.

Tips for refrigerator cookies: Chill dough until firm enough to slice easily. Use sharp knife.

About Ingredients

Baking powder: Use double-action baking powder, not single-action, for the recipes in this book.

Cocoa: When the recipes call for cocoa, use the unsweetened kind; do not use instant cocoa mix.

Eggs: Sizes usually available are extra large, large and medium. Eggs used in the testing were large.

Flour: Use either regular or quick-mixing all-purpose flour. Many recipes also call for whole wheat flour. Drop cookies made with stone-ground flour may spread more and have a coarser texture than those made with regular whole wheat flour.

Shortening: When the recipes call for shortening, use the solid hydrogenated type sold in cans.

Margarine or butter: Use stick-type (not whipped).

Vegetable oil: Use oil when called for. Do not substitute oil for solid or melted shortenings.

Measure—the Right Way

- Graduated Measuring Spoons: Pour or scoop dry ingredients into spoon until full; then level. Pour liquid into spoon until full.

- Graduated Measuring Cups: To measure flour and granulated sugar, fill, then level. Do not sift flour. To measure powdered sugar and buttermilk baking mix, lightly spoon into cup, then level. Sift powdered sugar only if it is lumpy. To measure nuts, coconut and cut-up or small fruit, spoon into cup and pack down lightly. To measure brown sugar, fats and shortening, spoon into cup and pack down firmly.

- Liquid Measuring Cup: Pour in liquid; read the measurement at eye level.

How to Store Cookies

■ Store crisp, thin cookies in a container with a loose-fitting cover. If they soften, heat in a 300° oven 3 to 5 minutes to recrisp. Store soft cookies in a tightly covered container. If replaced frequently, a piece of bread or apple in the container helps to keep the cookies soft.

How to Freeze Cookies

■ Frosted cookies can be frozen from 2 to 3 months. Freeze them uncovered until they are firm, then pack in a single layer in a plastic-wrap- or foil-lined airtight container. Seal the lining, close container, label and freeze. If freezing frosted and unfrosted cookies in the same container, use the shorter freezing time required by frosted cookies.

■ Unfrosted cookies can be frozen from 9 to 12 months. Thoroughly cool them as you would frosted cookies, but be sure to separate layers of cookies with wrap. Then seal wrap, close box, label and freeze.

■ Frozen cookies thaw very quickly. Just let them stand uncovered on serving plate for about 20 minutes.

■ To store rolls of refrigerator cookie dough, wrap and freeze. Frozen dough keeps 5 to 6 months. When ready to bake, slice the frozen dough with a sharp knife.

How to Pack and Mail Cookies

■ Choose any of the Cookies That Travel Well listed on this page. Or Fudge Brownie Mix (15.5 ounces), which can be baked in a 9-inch disposable foil pan, and Date Bar Mix (14 ounces), which can be baked in an 8-inch disposable foil pan, following package directions. These can be cut, wrapped and mailed in the pans they are baked in.

■ Accumulate a variety of cookies to send by freezing a dozen each time you bake cookies for your family.

■ Cut rolled cookies with rounded (not pointed) cutters to avoid crumbling and breakage. For added protection in mailing, cut them only slightly smaller in circumference than a soup or fruit juice can. Then wrap them in pairs and place them in the can to mail.

■ Or wrap in pairs or singly and pack in coffee or shortening cans (with reclosable plastic covers), shoe boxes, gift boxes or decorated metal tins. (See photographs on page 28.)

■ Fill each container as full as practical, padding the top with crushed paper to prevent shaking or breakage.

■ Pack containers in a foil-lined corrugated or fiberboard packing box. For filler, use crumpled newspapers, shredded paper or shredded polyethylene foam, which can be bought in fabric or notion departments.

■ Warning: Do not use popcorn or cereal products as filler. They can absorb noxious fumes from airplane engines and become unsafe to eat.

■ Seal packing box with tape; wrap tightly in heavy paper; tie with a strong cord.

■ Address in large, legible print directly on the package or on a gummed mailing label. Cover address with transparent tape to protect it from becoming blurred.

Cookies That Travel Well

Cookie Clinic

Problem: Dry Cookie Dough
Solution:
• Measure accurately. You don't want too much flour or too little liquid or shortening.
• Use room-temperature shortening, not chilled or melted.
• Use large eggs, the size used for testing these recipes. Don't use small eggs.
• Mix the cookie dough thoroughly. Be careful not to undermix!
Help!: If your dough is too dry, add 1 or 2 tablespoons cream or milk.

Problem: Dough Too Soft to Shape or Roll
Solution:
• Measure accurately. You don't want too little flour or too much liquid or shortening.
• Use shortening at room temperature, but not melted, and do not substitute oil.
• Use large eggs, not extra large.
• If it's a refrigerator dough, be sure it is firm enough to handle, then work with small amounts, leaving the rest in the refrigerator.
Help!: If your dough is too soft, mix in 1 or 2 tablespoons flour.

How Much Is Enough?
(Equivalents for Cookie Ingredients)

FOOD	IF YOU HAVE . . .	YOU'LL GET ABOUT . . .
Apricots, dried	1 pound	3 cups
Baking chocolate, unsweetened	8-ounce package	8 squares
Buttermilk baking mix	60-ounce package	13 cups
Cheese, cream	8-ounce package	1 cup
	3-ounce package	6 tablespoons
Cherries, maraschino	10-ounce jar	33 cherries
Chocolate chips	6-ounce package	1 cup
Coconut, shredded or flaked	4-ounce can	1⅓ cups
Cranberries, fresh	1 pound	4 cups
Dates, pitted, cut up	1 pound	2½ cups
Figs, dried, snipped	1 pound	2⅔ cups
Flour, all-purpose	1 pound	3½ cups
Flour, whole wheat	1 pound	3⅓ cups
Lemon peel, lightly grated	1 medium lemon	1½ to 3 teaspoons
Margarine or other shortening	1 pound	2 cups
Milk, sweetened condensed	14-ounce can	1⅓ cups
Nuts, shelled		
almonds	1 pound	3½ cups
peanuts	1 pound	3 cups
pecans	1 pound	4 cups
walnuts	1 pound	6¼ cups
Orange peel, lightly grated	1 medium orange	1 to 2 tablespoons
Prunes, dried, whole, pitted	1 pound	2¼ cups
Raisins, seedless	1 pound	2¾ cups
Sour cream, dairy	8-ounce carton	1 cup
Sugar, brown	1 pound	1¼ cups packed

Bar Cookies

Brownies

2 squares (1 ounce each) unsweetened
   chocolate
⅓ cup shortening
1 cup sugar
2 eggs
½ teaspoon vanilla
¾ cup all-purpose* or whole wheat flour
½ teaspoon baking powder
½ teaspoon salt
½ cup chopped nuts

Heat oven to 350°. Heat chocolate and shortening in 2-quart saucepan over low heat until melted; remove from heat. Mix in sugar, eggs and vanilla. Stir in remaining ingredients. Spread in greased baking pan, 8x8x2 inches. Bake until brownies begin to pull away from sides of pan, 30 to 35 minutes; cool. Cut into 1-inch squares.   ABOUT 4 DOZEN.

*If using self-rising flour, omit baking powder and salt.

Chocolate Peppermint Brownies: Immediately after removing from oven, place about 8 chocolate peppermint patties on brownies. Return pan to oven for several minutes until patties are softened; spread evenly.

Peanut Butter Brownies: Decrease shortening to 2 tablespoons and omit nuts. Stir in 2 tablespoons peanut butter and ¼ cup chopped peanuts with the remaining ingredients.

Quick Brownie Dress-ups

Prepare 1 package (15 ounces) fudge brownie mix as directed except—

Almond Brownies: Stir in ½ teaspoon almond extract.

Cashew Brownies: Sprinkle dough with ½ cup chopped salted cashews before baking.

Cherry Brownies: Stir in ¼ cup chopped maraschino cherries (about 16), well drained.

Coconut Brownies: Stir in 1 cup flaked or shredded coconut.

Crunchy Brownies: Stir in 3 tablespoons crunchy peanut butter.

Date Brownies: Stir in 1 cup cut-up dates. Roll brownies in powdered sugar.

Holiday Fruit Brownies: Stir in ⅓ cup cut-up candied fruit.

Mint Brownies: Stir in ½ cup semisweet mint chocolate chips.

Mocha Brownies: Stir 1 tablespoon plus 1½ teaspoons powdered instant coffee into brownie mix (dry).

Orange Brownies: Substitute orange juice for the water and stir in grated peel of 1 orange.

Peanut Brownies: Stir in ½ cup chopped peanuts.

Peppermint Brownies: Stir in ¼ teaspoon peppermint extract.

Marbled Brownies

Cream Cheese Filling (below)
1 cup margarine or butter
4 squares (1 ounce each) unsweetened chocolate
2 cups sugar
4 eggs
2 teaspoons vanilla
1½ cups all-purpose flour *
½ teaspoon salt
1 cup coarsely chopped nuts

Heat oven to 350°. Prepare Cream Cheese Filling. Heat margarine and chocolate over low heat until melted; cool. Beat chocolate mixture, sugar, eggs and vanilla in large mixer bowl on medium speed, scraping bowl occasionally, about 1 minute. Beat in flour and salt on low speed, scraping bowl occasionally, about 30 seconds. Beat on medium speed about 1 minute. Stir in nuts.

Spread half of the batter in greased baking pan, 9x9x2 inches. Spread with Cream Cheese Filling. Lightly spread remaining batter over Cream Cheese Filling. Gently swirl through batter with spoon in an over-and-under motion for marbled effect. Bake until wooden pick inserted in center comes out clean, 55 to 65 minutes; cool. Cut into bars, 2x1 inch.   ABOUT 3 DOZEN.

*If using self-rising flour, omit salt. Bake in greased baking pan, 13x9x2 inches, 40 to 45 minutes; cool. Cut into bars, about 1½x1 inch.   ABOUT 5 DOZEN.

CREAM CHEESE FILLING

1 package (8 ounces) cream cheese, softened
¼ cup sugar
1 teaspoon ground cinnamon
1 egg
1½ teaspoons vanilla

Beat all ingredients in small mixer bowl, scraping bowl occasionally, about 2 minutes.

Fudgy Brownies

½ cup margarine or butter
2 squares (1 ounce each) unsweetened chocolate
1 cup sugar
2 eggs
1 teaspoon vanilla
½ cup all-purpose flour *
¼ teaspoon salt
½ cup chopped walnuts

Heat oven to 350°. Heat margarine and chocolate in 2-quart saucepan over low heat until melted; remove from heat. Mix in sugar, eggs and vanilla. Stir in remaining ingredients. Spread in greased baking pan, 9x9x2 inches. Bake until brownies begin to pull away from sides of pan, 20 to 25 minutes; cool. Cut into 1-inch squares.   ABOUT 5 DOZEN.

*If using self-rising flour, omit salt.

Meringue-topped Brownies

2 squares (1 ounce each) unsweetened chocolate
⅓ cup shortening
1 cup sugar
1 egg
1 egg yolk
¾ cup all-purpose flour
½ teaspoon baking powder
½ teaspoon salt
Meringue (below)

Heat oven to 350°. Heat chocolate and shortening in 2-quart saucepan over low heat until melted; remove from heat. Stir in sugar. Beat in egg and egg yolk. Mix in flour, baking powder and salt. Spread in well-greased baking pan, 9x9x2 inches. Prepare Meringue; spread over mixture in pan. Bake 30 to 35 minutes; cool. Cut into 2-inch squares.   ABOUT 1½ DOZEN.

MERINGUE

Beat 1 egg white in small mixer bowl until foamy. Beat in 1 cup packed brown sugar gradually; continue beating until stiff and glossy. Do not underbeat. Beat in ½ teaspoon vanilla. Fold in ½ cup chopped nuts.

Double-frosted Brownies

Pictured on page 18.

> Fudgy Brownies (page 8)
> 1½ cups powdered sugar
> ½ cup whipping cream
> ⅓ cup margarine or butter
> 1 teaspoon vanilla
> 3 ounces melted unsweetened chocolate
> (cool)

Prepare Fudgy Brownies; cool. Heat powdered sugar, whipping cream and margarine to boiling in 2-quart saucepan over medium heat, stirring constantly. Boil, without stirring, until candy thermometer registers 234° or until small amount of mixture dropped into very cold water forms a soft ball that flattens when removed from water; cool slightly. Beat in vanilla until smooth and of spreading consistency; spread over brownies. Spread chocolate over frosting. Refrigerate until chocolate is set. (Refrigerate until 1 hour before serving in warm weather.) Cut into 1-inch squares.   ABOUT 5 DOZEN.

Cocoa Brownies

> 1 cup sugar
> ½ cup shortening
> 2 eggs
> 1 teaspoon vanilla
> ⅔ cup all-purpose flour
> ½ cup cocoa
> ½ teaspoon baking powder
> ½ teaspoon salt
> ½ cup chopped walnuts

Heat oven to 350°. Mix sugar, shortening, eggs and vanilla. Stir in remaining ingredients. Spread in well-greased baking pan, 8x8x2 inches. Bake until wooden pick inserted in center comes out clean, 25 to 30 minutes; cool. Cut into 1-inch squares.   ABOUT 4 DOZEN.

For Special Times

Chocolate-Date Squares

> 1½ cups cut-up dates
> ¾ cup water
> 2 tablespoons granulated sugar
> ½ square (½ ounce) unsweetened chocolate
> ½ cup packed brown sugar
> ⅓ cup margarine or butter, softened
> ¾ cup all-purpose flour *
> ½ teaspoon salt
> ¼ teaspoon baking soda
> ¾ cup oats
> ⅓ cup chopped nuts

Heat oven to 400°. Cook dates, water, granulated sugar and chocolate over low heat, stirring constantly, until mixture thickens, about 10 minutes; cool.

Mix brown sugar and margarine. Stir in remaining ingredients. Press half of the crumbly mixture in greased baking pan, 8x8x2 inches. Spread with date mixture; top with remaining crumbly mixture, pressing lightly. Bake until golden brown, 25 to 30 minutes; cool. Cut into 1¾-inch squares.   ABOUT 1½ DOZEN.

*If using self-rising flour, omit salt and baking soda.

Granola Chocolate-Date Squares: Decrease flour to ½ cup and omit baking soda. Substitute 1 cup granola for the oats. Bake 20 to 25 minutes.

Chocolate-Applesauce Bars

½ cup shortening
2 squares (1 ounce each) unsweetened chocolate
1 cup sugar
1 cup all-purpose flour*
½ cup applesauce
2 eggs
1 teaspoon vanilla
½ teaspoon baking powder
¼ teaspoon baking soda
¼ teaspoon salt
½ cup chopped nuts

Heat oven to 350°. Heat shortening and chocolate over low heat until melted; remove from heat. Stir in remaining ingredients. Spread in greased and floured baking pan, 9x9x2 inches. Bake until top springs back when touched, 35 to 40 minutes. Cut into bars, 2x1 inch, while warm.   ABOUT 3 DOZEN.

*If using self-rising flour, omit baking powder, baking soda and salt.

Milk Chocolate Bars

1 cup packed brown sugar
½ cup margarine or butter
½ cup milk
2 eggs, beaten
1¼ cups all-purpose flour*
1 teaspoon salt
1 teaspoon baking powder
¼ teaspoon baking soda
1 package (6 ounces) semisweet chocolate chips
1 cup coarsely chopped nuts

Heat oven to 350°. Mix brown sugar, margarine and milk in saucepan. Heat to boiling, stirring constantly; remove from heat. Cool 5 minutes; stir in eggs. Mix in flour, salt, baking powder and baking soda. Stir in chocolate chips and nuts. Spread in greased and floured baking pan, 13x9x2 inches. Bake 25 minutes; cool. Cut into bars, 2x1 inch.   4 DOZEN.

*If using self-rising flour, omit salt, baking powder and baking soda.

Choco-Dot Chewies

1 cup all-purpose flour*
½ cup packed brown sugar
¼ cup shortening
3 tablespoons milk
⅛ teaspoon salt
2 eggs, beaten
¾ cup packed brown sugar
1 teaspoon vanilla
¼ teaspoon salt
1 cup shredded coconut
1 cup chopped nuts
1 package (6 ounces) semisweet chocolate chips

Heat oven to 350°. Mix flour, ½ cup brown sugar, the shortening, milk and ⅛ teaspoon salt. Press in greased baking pan, 13x9x2 inches. Bake 10 minutes.

Beat eggs; stir in remaining ingredients. Spread over baked layer. Bake 20 minutes. Cut into bars, 2x1 inch, while warm.   4 DOZEN.

*If using self-rising flour, omit salt in base.

Chocolate Chip-Fruit Bars

1¼ cups all-purpose flour*
1 cup sugar
3 eggs
1½ teaspoons baking powder
1 teaspoon salt
½ teaspoon almond extract
1 package (6 ounces) semisweet chocolate chips
1 cup cut-up dates or whole raisins
1 cup chopped nuts
½ cup chopped maraschino cherries, drained

Heat oven to 350°. Mix all ingredients. Spread in greased baking pan, 13x9x2 inches. Bake until light brown, 30 to 35 minutes; cool. Frost with Browned Butter Frosting (page 20) if desired. Cut into bars, 2x1 inch.   4 DOZEN.

*If using self-rising flour, omit baking powder and salt.

Chocolate Chip Squares

1¼ cups packed brown sugar
⅓ cup shortening
2 eggs
1¼ cups all-purpose flour *
1¼ teaspoons baking powder
¼ teaspoon salt
½ cup semisweet chocolate chips
½ cup coarsely chopped nuts

Heat oven to 350°. Mix brown sugar, shortening and eggs. Stir in remaining ingredients. Spread in greased baking pan, 9x9x2 inches. Bake until light brown, about 30 minutes; cool. Cut into 2-inch squares.   ABOUT 1½ DOZEN.

*If using self-rising flour, omit baking powder and salt.

Quick Oatmeal-Fudge Bars

2 cups packed brown sugar
¾ cup margarine or butter, softened
2 eggs
2 teaspoons vanilla
2½ cups buttermilk baking mix
3 cups quick-cooking oats
1 package (12 ounces) semisweet chocolate chips
1 cup sweetened condensed milk
2 tablespoons margarine or butter
½ teaspoon salt
1 cup chopped nuts
2 teaspoons vanilla

Heat oven to 350°. Mix brown sugar, ¾ cup margarine, the eggs and 2 teaspoons vanilla. Stir in baking mix and oats until of uniform consistency. Heat chocolate chips, milk, 2 tablespoons margarine and the salt in 2-quart saucepan over low heat, stirring constantly, until smooth. Stir in nuts and 2 teaspoons vanilla.

Press about ⅔ of the oatmeal mixture in greased jelly roll pan, 15½x10½x1 inch, with greased hands. Spread chocolate mixture over oatmeal layer. Drop remaining oatmeal mixture by tablespoonfuls onto top. Bake until light brown, about 30 minutes; cool completely. Cut into bars, 2x1 inch.   ABOUT 5 DOZEN.

Oatmeal-Chocolate Chip Squares

⅔ cup packed brown sugar
⅓ cup shortening
1 egg
½ cup milk
1 cup all-purpose flour *
½ teaspoon salt
¼ teaspoon baking soda
1¼ cups quick-cooking oats
1 package (6 ounces) semisweet chocolate chips
Orange Glaze (below)

Heat oven to 350°. Mix brown sugar, shortening and egg. Stir in milk. Mix in flour, salt, baking soda, oats and chocolate chips. Spread in greased baking pan, 9x9x2 inches. Bake until firm, about 25 minutes. Immediately spread with Orange Glaze; cool. Cut into 2-inch squares. ABOUT 1½ DOZEN.

*If using self-rising flour, omit salt and baking soda.

ORANGE GLAZE
Beat 1 cup powdered sugar, 2 tablespoons margarine or butter, softened, 2 teaspoons grated orange peel and 1 tablespoon orange juice until of desired consistency.

Layered Granola Bars

⅓ cup margarine or butter
3 cups granola, slightly crushed
1 package (6 ounces) semisweet chocolate chips
½ cup flaked or shredded coconut
½ cup slivered almonds
1 can (14 ounces) sweetened condensed milk

Heat oven to 325°. Heat margarine in baking pan, 13x9x2 inches, in oven until melted. Rotate pan until margarine covers bottom; sprinkle with granola. Bake 15 minutes.

Sprinkle chocolate chips, coconut and almonds over granola. Pour milk over top. Bake until light brown, about 20 minutes. Loosen edges from sides of pan while warm; cool. Cut into bars, 2x1 inch.   4 DOZEN.

Chocolate Swirl Bars

½ cup packed brown sugar
½ cup margarine or butter, softened
1 egg
1 teaspoon vanilla
1¼ cups all-purpose flour
½ teaspoon baking soda
½ teaspoon salt
2 cups granola, slightly crushed
  Chocolate Filling (below)

Heat oven to 350°. Mix brown sugar, margarine, egg and vanilla. Stir in flour, baking soda, salt and granola. Press ⅔ of the granola mixture in greased baking pan, 13x9x2 inches. Spread with Chocolate Filling. Drop remaining granola mixture by teaspoonfuls onto Chocolate Filling; spread in swirl design. Bake until granola mixture is light brown, about 25 minutes; cool. Cut into bars, 2x1 inch.   4 DOZEN.

CHOCOLATE FILLING
1 package (6 ounces) semisweet chocolate chips
½ cup sweetened condensed milk
1 tablespoon margarine or butter
¼ teaspoon salt
1 teaspoon vanilla
½ cup chopped pecans

Mix chocolate chips, milk, margarine and salt in saucepan. Cook over low heat, stirring constantly, until chocolate is melted and mixture is smooth; remove from heat. Stir in vanilla and pecans.

Quick and Easy

Chocolate Peanut Butter Bars

Pictured on page 17.

½ cup granulated sugar
½ cup packed brown sugar
½ cup shortening
½ cup peanut butter
1 egg
2 tablespoons water
1¼ cups all-purpose flour*
¾ teaspoon baking soda
½ teaspoon baking powder
¼ teaspoon salt
1 package (6 ounces) semisweet chocolate chips
  Chocolate Glaze (below)
½ cup chopped salted peanuts

Heat oven to 375°. Mix sugars, shortening, peanut butter and egg. Stir in water, flour, baking soda, baking powder, salt and chocolate chips. Spread in greased baking pan, 13x9x2 inches. Bake about 20 minutes. Spread with Chocolate Glaze while warm; sprinkle with peanuts. Cut into bars, 1½x1 inch.   ABOUT 6 DOZEN.

*If using self-rising flour, omit baking soda, baking powder and salt.

CHOCOLATE GLAZE
2 squares (1 ounce each) unsweetened chocolate
3 tablespoons margarine or butter
1 cup powdered sugar
¾ teaspoon vanilla
  About 2 tablespoons hot water

Heat chocolate and margarine over low heat until melted; remove from heat. Stir in powdered sugar and vanilla. Beat in water, 1 teaspoon at a time, until smooth and of desired consistency.

Chocolate-Almond Squares

2 cups all-purpose flour*
1 cup sugar
1 cup margarine or butter, softened
1 egg
½ teaspoon almond extract
½ cup roasted diced almonds
2 ounces melted semisweet or sweet
    cooking chocolate (cool)

Heat oven to 325°. Beat flour, sugar, margarine, egg, almond extract and almonds until dough forms. Spread in greased baking pan, 13x9x2 inches. Bake until golden brown, 35 to 40 minutes. Drizzle with chocolate; cool slightly. Cut into 1-inch squares.   8 DOZEN.

*Self-rising flour can be used in this recipe.

Coffee-Cinnamon Bars

1 cup packed brown sugar
¼ cup shortening
1 egg
½ cup water
1½ cups all-purpose flour*
2 tablespoons powdered instant coffee
1 teaspoon baking powder
½ teaspoon ground cinnamon
¼ teaspoon salt
¼ teaspoon baking soda
½ cup raisins
¼ cup chopped nuts
    Glaze (below)

Heat oven to 350°. Mix brown sugar, shortening and egg. Stir in remaining ingredients except Glaze. Spread in greased and floured baking pan, 13x9x2 inches. Bake 18 to 20 minutes. Drizzle with Glaze while warm. Cut into bars, 3x1 inch.   ABOUT 3 DOZEN.

*If using self-rising flour, omit baking powder and salt.

GLAZE
Beat 1 cup powdered sugar, ¼ teaspoon vanilla and about 1 tablespoon plus 1½ teaspoons milk until smooth and of desired consistency.

Toffee-Coconut Bars

½ cup packed brown sugar
¼ cup margarine or butter, softened
¼ cup shortening
1 cup all-purpose flour*
    Coconut-Almond Topping or
    Coconut-Lemon Topping (below)

Heat oven to 350°. Mix brown sugar, margarine and shortening. Stir in flour. Press in ungreased baking pan, 13x9x2 inches. Bake 10 minutes.

Spread Coconut-Almond Topping over baked layer. Bake until golden brown, about 25 minutes; cool slightly. Cut into bars, 3x1 inch.   ABOUT 3 DOZEN.

*If using self-rising flour, omit baking powder and salt in topping.

COCONUT-ALMOND TOPPING
2 eggs
1 cup packed brown sugar
2 tablespoons flour
1 teaspoon baking powder
1 teaspoon vanilla
½ teaspoon salt
1 cup shredded coconut
1 cup chopped almonds

Beat eggs; stir in remaining ingredients.

COCONUT-LEMON TOPPING
2 eggs
1 cup packed brown sugar
1 teaspoon grated lemon peel
2 tablespoons lemon juice
½ teaspoon salt
1 cup shredded coconut
1 cup cut-up raisins
1 cup chopped walnuts

Beat eggs; stir in remaining ingredients.

Chewy Butterscotch Squares

    1   cup granulated sugar
    ½   cup shortening
    1   egg
    1   egg, separated
    1   teaspoon vanilla
    1¼ cups all-purpose flour*
    1   teaspoon baking powder
    ½   teaspoon salt
    1   cup packed brown sugar
    ½   cup chopped nuts

Heat oven to 375°. Beat granulated sugar, shortening, egg, egg yolk and vanilla in large mixer bowl until blended. Stir in flour, baking powder and salt. Pat in greased baking pan, 13x9x2 inches.

Beat egg white in small mixer bowl until foamy; beat in brown sugar gradually; continue beating until stiff and glossy. Do not underbeat. Fold in nuts. Spread carefully over layer in pan. Bake until golden brown, about 25 minutes. Cut into 2-inch squares while warm.   2 DOZEN.

*If using self-rising flour, omit baking powder and salt. Bake about 20 minutes.

Butterscotch Brownies

Pictured on page 79.

    ¼   cup shortening or vegetable oil
    1   cup packed brown sugar
    1   egg
    1   teaspoon vanilla
    ¾   cup all-purpose* or whole wheat flour
    1   teaspoon baking powder
    ½   teaspoon salt
    ½   cup chopped nuts

Heat oven to 350°. Heat shortening over low heat until melted; remove from heat. Mix in brown sugar, egg and vanilla. Stir in remaining ingredients. Spread in greased baking pan, 8x8x2 inches. Bake 25 minutes. Cut into 1¾-inch squares while warm.   ABOUT 1½ DOZEN.

*If using self-rising flour, omit baking powder and salt.

Brazil Nut Brownies: Substitute ¾ cup ground Brazil nuts for the chopped nuts.

Butterscotch-Date Brownies: Decrease vanilla to ½ teaspoon. Stir in ½ cup snipped dates with the remaining ingredients.

Coconut-Butterscotch Brownies: Decrease vanilla to ½ teaspoon. Substitute cookie coconut for the nuts.

Cookie Cutter Butterscotch Brownies: Decrease vanilla to ½ teaspoon. Substitute ½ cup broken nuts for the chopped nuts. Spread in greased baking pan, 13x9x2 inches. Sprinkle with ¼ cup finely chopped nuts. Bake 15 minutes (do not overbake). Cut with 1½-inch round or fancy cookie cutters while warm.

Spicy Toffee Triangles

    1   cup packed brown sugar
    1   cup margarine or butter, softened
    1   egg, separated
    1   teaspoon vanilla
    2   cups all-purpose flour*
    ¼   teaspoon salt
    1   teaspoon ground cinnamon
    1   cup chopped walnuts

Heat oven to 275°. Mix brown sugar, margarine, egg yolk and vanilla. Stir in flour, salt and cinnamon. Spread in ungreased jelly roll pan, 15½x10½x1 inch. Brush dough with unbeaten egg white. Sprinkle with walnuts; press lightly. Bake 1 hour. While warm, cut into 2½-inch squares, then cut each square diagonally into halves; cool.   ABOUT 4 DOZEN.

*If using self-rising flour, omit salt.

Greek Triangles: Substitute ground cardamom for the cinnamon and 1 can (5 ounces) diced roasted almonds for the walnuts.

Hawaiian Spice Triangles: Substitute ground ginger for the cinnamon and ¼ cup chopped salted macadamia nuts and ¼ cup flaked coconut for the walnuts.

Orange-Chocolate Triangles: Substitute ½ teaspoon ground cloves and 1 tablespoon grated orange peel for the cinnamon and 2 packages (6 ounces each) semisweet chocolate chips for the walnuts.

Mixed Nut Squares

1 cup packed brown sugar
1 cup margarine or butter, softened
1 egg yolk
1 teaspoon vanilla
2 cups all-purpose* or whole wheat flour
¼ teaspoon salt
1 package (6 ounces) butterscotch chips
½ cup light corn syrup
2 tablespoons margarine or butter
1 tablespoon water
1 can (13 ounces) salted mixed nuts

Heat oven to 350°. Mix brown sugar, 1 cup margarine, the egg yolk and vanilla. Stir in flour and salt. Press in ungreased baking pan, 13x9x2 inches. Bake until light brown, about 25 minutes; cool.

Mix butterscotch chips, corn syrup, 2 tablespoons margarine and the water in saucepan. Cook over medium heat, stirring occasionally, until butterscotch is melted; cool. Spread over baked layer. Sprinkle with nuts, pressing lightly. Refrigerate until topping is firm, about 1 hour. Cut into 2-inch squares. Store in refrigerator. 2 DOZEN.

*Do not use self-rising flour in this recipe.

Filbert Bars

1 cup sugar
1 cup margarine or butter, softened
1 egg, separated
1½ cups all-purpose flour*
¼ teaspoon salt
1 cup finely chopped filberts

Heat oven to 275°. Mix sugar, margarine and egg yolk. Stir in flour and salt. Spread in ungreased jelly roll pan, 15½x10½x1 inch. Beat egg white slightly; brush over dough. Sprinkle filberts over top, pressing lightly. Bake until golden brown, about 1 hour. Immediately cut into bars, 2x1 inch; cool. Store in tightly covered container. ABOUT 5 DOZEN.

*If using self-rising flour, omit salt.

Molasses Taffy Bars

1½ cups all-purpose flour*
¾ cup packed brown sugar
½ cup margarine or butter, softened
¼ cup dark molasses
2 eggs
½ teaspoon salt
½ teaspoon ground ginger
½ teaspoon ground cinnamon
¼ teaspoon baking soda
1 cup chopped pecans
Orange-Lemon Frosting (page 16)

Heat oven to 350°. Grease bottom only of baking pan, 13x9x2 inches. Beat all ingredients except frosting in large mixer bowl on low speed, scraping bowl constantly, 30 seconds. Beat on medium speed, scraping bowl frequently, 1 minute. Spread in pan. Bake until light brown, about 25 minutes; cool. Frost with Orange-Lemon Frosting. Cut into bars, 2x1 inch. 4 DOZEN.

*If using self-rising flour, omit salt and baking soda.

Chewy Sesame Bars

½ cup sesame seed
1½ cups packed brown sugar
⅓ cup margarine or butter, softened
2 eggs
1 cup all-purpose flour*
1 teaspoon ground mace or cinnamon
½ teaspoon salt
½ teaspoon baking soda

Heat oven to 350°. Spread sesame seed in ungreased baking pan. Bake, stirring once, until toasted, 10 minutes.

Mix brown sugar, margarine and eggs. Stir in flour, mace, salt and baking soda. Sprinkle half of the sesame seed in ungreased baking pan, 13x9x2 inches. Beginning at center of pan, spread dough over seed; sprinkle with remaining seed. Bake until dough begins to pull away from sides of pan, about 25 minutes; cool slightly. Cut into bars, about 2x1 inch. Store in airtight container. 4 DOZEN.

*Self-rising flour can be used in this recipe.

Cinnamon Strips

Also called *Jan Hagel,* these cookie strips with a baked-on glaze originated in Holland.

```
1   cup sugar
1   cup margarine or butter, softened
1   egg, separated
2   cups all-purpose flour*
½   teaspoon ground cinnamon
1   tablespoon water
½   cup very finely chopped walnuts
```

Heat oven to 350°. Mix sugar, margarine and egg yolk. Stir in flour and cinnamon. Press in lightly greased jelly roll pan, 15½x10½x1 inch. (Or use 2 baking pans, one 8x8x2 inches and one 9x9x2 inches.) Beat egg white and water until foamy; brush over dough. Sprinkle with walnuts. Bake until very light brown, 20 to 25 minutes. Immediately cut into strips, 3x1 inch. 3½ DOZEN.

*Self-rising flour can be used in this recipe.

Coconut-Cherry Bars

Pictured at right.

```
1   cup all-purpose flour*
½   cup margarine or butter, softened
3   tablespoons powdered sugar
2   eggs
1   cup granulated sugar
¼   cup all-purpose flour*
1   teaspoon vanilla
½   teaspoon baking powder
¼   teaspoon salt
¾   cup chopped nuts
½   cup flaked coconut
½   cup chopped maraschino cherries,
      drained
```

Heat oven to 350°. Mix 1 cup flour, the margarine and powdered sugar. Press in greased baking pan, 8x8x2 or 9x9x2 inches. Bake 10 minutes.

Beat eggs; stir in remaining ingredients. Spread over baked layer. Bake until golden brown, 25 to 30 minutes; cool. Cut into bars, 2x1 inch. ABOUT 2 DOZEN.

*If using self-rising flour, omit baking powder and salt.

Coconut Chews

```
¾    cup powdered sugar
¾    cup shortening (half margarine or
       butter, softened)
1½   cups all-purpose* or whole wheat flour
1    cup packed brown sugar
2    eggs
2    tablespoons flour
½    teaspoon baking powder
½    teaspoon salt
½    teaspoon vanilla
½    cup chopped walnuts
½    cup flaked coconut
```

Heat oven to 350°. Mix powdered sugar and shortening. Stir in 1½ cups flour. Press in ungreased baking pan, 13x9x2 inches. Bake 12 to 15 minutes.

Mix remaining ingredients. Spread over baked layer. Bake 20 minutes; cool. Frost with Orange-Lemon Frosting or Chocolate Frosting (below) if desired. Cut into bars, 3x1 inch. ABOUT 3 DOZEN.

*Self-rising flour can be used in this recipe.

ORANGE-LEMON FROSTING
Mix 1½ cups powdered sugar, 2 tablespoons margarine or butter, melted, 3 tablespoons orange juice and 1 teaspoon lemon juice.

CHOCOLATE FROSTING
```
2    tablespoons shortening
2    squares (1 ounce each) unsweetened
       chocolate
1½   cups powdered sugar
⅛    teaspoon salt
3    tablespoons milk
½    teaspoon vanilla
```

Heat shortening and chocolate over low heat until melted. Stir in remaining ingredients; beat until smooth.

Pecan Chews: Substitute 1 cup chopped pecans for the walnuts and coconut.

Bar cookies—Pumpkin (page 22), Chocolate Peanut Butter (page 12) and Coconut-Cherry (page 16)

18

Chocolate cookies—Chocolate Drops (page 45), Double-frosted Brownies (page 9), Caramel-Oat Bars (page 19) and Chocolate Cookie Slices (page 83)

Coconut-Apricot Bars

½ cup powdered sugar
¼ cup margarine or butter, softened
¼ cup shortening
2 eggs, separated
1 cup all-purpose flour*
½ cup granulated sugar
½ cup flaked coconut
1 cup apricot preserves

Heat oven to 350°. Beat powdered sugar, margarine, shortening and egg yolks in small mixer bowl until blended. Stir in flour. Press in ungreased baking pan, 13x9x2 inches. Bake 10 minutes.

Beat egg whites in small mixer bowl until foamy. Beat in granulated sugar, 1 tablespoon at a time; continue beating until stiff and glossy. Do not underbeat. Fold in coconut. Spread preserves over baked layer. Spread meringue carefully over preserves. Bake until topping is golden brown, about 20 minutes; cool slightly. Cut into bars, 2x1 inch.   4 DOZEN.

*Self-rising flour can be used in this recipe.

Coconut-Orange Bars

1 cup packed brown sugar
¼ cup shortening
¼ cup margarine or butter, softened
1 egg
2 tablespoons milk
½ teaspoon vanilla
¼ teaspoon lemon extract
1 cup all-purpose flour*
2 teaspoons baking powder
½ teaspoon salt
⅓ cup shredded coconut
2 tablespoons snipped candied orange peel

Heat oven to 325°. Mix brown sugar, shortening, margarine, egg, milk, vanilla and lemon extract. Stir in remaining ingredients. Spread in lightly greased baking pan, 9x9x2 inches. Bake until light brown, 30 to 35 minutes. Cut into bars, 2x1 inch, while warm.   ABOUT 3 DOZEN.

*If using self-rising flour, omit baking powder and salt.

Caramel-Oat Bars

Pictured at left.

2 cups oats
½ cup packed brown sugar
½ cup margarine or butter, melted
¼ cup dark corn syrup
1 teaspoon vanilla
½ teaspoon salt
1 package (6 ounces) semisweet chocolate chips

Heat oven to 400°. Mix oats, brown sugar, margarine, corn syrup, vanilla and salt. Spread in greased baking pan, 9x9x2 inches. Bake until bubbly, about 8 minutes. Immediately sprinkle with chocolate chips. Let stand until soft; spread evenly. Sprinkle with chopped nuts if desired. Refrigerate at least 1 hour. Cut into bars, 2x1 inch. Store in refrigerator.   ABOUT 3 DOZEN.

Oatmeal Bars

1 cup margarine or butter, softened
½ cup granulated sugar
½ cup packed brown sugar
2 egg yolks
1 cup all-purpose flour*
1 cup oats
6 bars (1.05 ounces each) milk chocolate candy
2 tablespoons margarine or butter
½ cup chopped nuts

Heat oven to 350°. Mix 1 cup margarine, the sugars and egg yolks. Stir in flour and oats. Spread in greased and floured baking pan, 13x9x2 inches. Bake until light brown, 20 to 25 minutes; cool 10 minutes.

Heat chocolate and 2 tablespoons margarine over low heat until melted; spread over baked layer. Sprinkle with nuts. Cut into bars, 2x1 inch.   4 DOZEN.

*Self-rising flour can be used in this recipe.

Date Bars

       Date Filling or Date-Apricot Filling
          (below)
   1 cup packed brown sugar
   ½ cup margarine or butter, softened
   ¼ cup shortening
   1¾ cups all-purpose* or whole wheat flour
   1 teaspoon salt
   ½ teaspoon baking soda
   1½ cups quick-cooking oats

Prepare Date Filling; cool. Heat oven to 400°. Mix brown sugar, margarine and shortening. Stir in remaining ingredients. Press half of the crumbly mixture in greased baking pan, 13x9x2 inches; spread with filling. Top with remaining crumbly mixture; press lightly. Bake until light brown, 25 to 30 minutes. Cut into bars, 2x1 inch, while warm.   4 DOZEN.

*If using self-rising flour, omit salt and baking soda.

DATE FILLING
Mix 1 package (16 ounces) dates, cut up (about 3 cups), 1½ cups water and ¼ cup sugar in saucepan. Cook over low heat, stirring constantly, until thickened, about 10 minutes.

DATE-APRICOT FILLING
Mix 1 package (8 ounces) dates, cut up (about 1½ cups), 1 package (8 ounces) dried apricots, cut up (about 1½ cups), 1½ cups water and ½ cup sugar. Cook over medium-low heat, stirring constantly, until thickened, about 10 minutes.

Fig-Nut Bars

   1½ cups snipped dried figs or 2 cups
          snipped dates
   ½ cup all-purpose flour*
   ½ cup sugar
   2 eggs
   ½ teaspoon baking powder
   ½ teaspoon salt
   ½ teaspoon vanilla
   1 cup chopped nuts

Heat oven to 350°. Mix all ingredients. Spread in greased baking pan, 9x9x2 inches. Bake until light brown, about 25 minutes. Cut into bars, 2x1 inch.   ABOUT 3 DOZEN.

*If using self-rising flour, omit baking powder and salt.

Quick Date Bars

       Date Filling (below)
   1 cup packed brown sugar
   ½ cup margarine or butter, softened
   ¼ cup shortening
   2 cups buttermilk baking mix
   1½ cups quick-cooking oats

Prepare Date Filling; cool. Heat oven to 400°. Mix brown sugar, margarine and shortening. Stir in baking mix and oats. Press half of the crumbly mixture in greased baking pan, 9x9x2 inches; spread with filling. Top with remaining crumbly mixture, pressing lightly. Bake until light brown, 25 to 30 minutes. Cut into bars, 2x1 inch. ABOUT 3 DOZEN.

DATE FILLING
Mix 1 package (8 ounces) dates, cut up (about 1½ cups), ¾ cup water and 2 tablespoons sugar in saucepan. Cook over low heat, stirring constantly, until thickened, about 5 minutes.

Applesauce-Spice Bars

   1 cup all-purpose flour*
   ⅔ cup packed brown sugar
   1 teaspoon baking soda
   ½ teaspoon salt
   1 teaspoon pumpkin pie spice
   1 cup applesauce
   ¼ cup shortening
   1 egg
   ½ cup raisins
       Browned Butter Frosting (below)

Heat oven to 350°. Mix all ingredients except frosting. Spread in greased baking pan, 13x9x2 inches. Bake about 25 minutes; cool. Frost with Browned Butter Frosting. Cut into bars, 3x1 inch.   ABOUT 3 DOZEN.

*If using self-rising flour, decrease baking soda to ½ teaspoon and omit salt.

BROWNED BUTTER FROSTING
Heat 3 tablespoons butter over medium heat until delicate brown; remove from heat. Beat in 1½ cups powdered sugar, 1 teaspoon vanilla and about 1 tablespoon milk until smooth and of spreading consistency.

Banana-Sour Cream Bars

1½ cups sugar
  1 cup dairy sour cream
  ½ cup margarine or butter, softened
  2 eggs
1½ cups mashed bananas (about 3 large)
  2 teaspoons vanilla
  2 cups all-purpose flour
  1 teaspoon salt
  1 teaspoon baking soda
  ½ cup chopped nuts
    Vanilla Glaze (right)

Heat oven to 375°. Mix sugar, sour cream, margarine and eggs in large mixer bowl on low speed, scraping bowl occasionally, 1 minute. Beat in bananas and vanilla on low speed 30 seconds. Beat in flour, salt and baking soda on medium speed, scraping bowl occasionally, 1 minute. Stir in nuts. Spread in greased and floured jelly roll pan, 15½x10½x1 inch. Bake until light brown, 20 to 25 minutes; cool. Frost with Vanilla Glaze. Cut into bars, 2x1 inch. ABOUT 6 DOZEN.

Lemon Squares

  1 cup all-purpose* or whole wheat flour
  ½ cup margarine or butter, softened
  ¼ cup powdered sugar
  1 cup granulated sugar
  2 eggs
  2 teaspoons grated lemon peel, if desired
  2 tablespoons lemon juice
  ½ teaspoon baking powder
  ¼ teaspoon salt

Heat oven to 350°. Mix flour, margarine and powdered sugar. Press in ungreased baking pan, 8x8x2 inches, building up ½-inch edges. Bake 20 minutes.

Beat remaining ingredients until light and fluffy, about 3 minutes; pour over baked layer. Bake until no indentation remains when touched in center, about 25 minutes; cool. Cut into 1-inch squares. ABOUT 4 DOZEN.

*If using self-rising flour, omit baking powder and salt.

Lemon-Coconut Squares: Stir ½ cup flaked coconut into egg mixture.

Orange-Oatmeal Bars

1¼ cups all-purpose flour*
  1 cup packed brown sugar
  ¾ cup oats
  ¾ cup margarine or butter, softened
  ½ cup flaked coconut
  1 tablespoon grated orange peel
  ½ teaspoon salt
  ¾ cup orange marmalade

Heat oven to 325°. Mix all ingredients except marmalade. Press half of the crumbly mixture in ungreased baking pan, 8x8x2 inches. Spread with marmalade; sprinkle with remaining crumbly mixture, pressing lightly. Bake about 40 minutes; cool. Cut into bars, 1¾x1 inch. ABOUT 2½ DOZEN.

*If using self-rising flour, omit salt.

Jeweled Bars

1¾ cups packed brown sugar
  4 eggs, separated
  1 teaspoon vanilla
  2 cups all-purpose flour*
  1 teaspoon baking powder
  ½ teaspoon salt
  1 cup snipped candied orange slices
    (about 13)
  ¾ cup chopped nuts
    Vanilla Glaze (below)

Heat oven to 350°. Mix brown sugar, egg yolks and vanilla. Stir in flour, baking powder, salt, orange slices and nuts. Beat egg whites until stiff but not dry; stir into egg yolk mixture. Spread in greased jelly roll pan, 15½x10½x1 inch. Bake until wooden pick inserted in center comes out clean, about 20 minutes; cool. Spread with Vanilla Glaze. Cut into bars, 2x1 inch. ABOUT 5 DOZEN.

*If using self-rising flour, omit baking powder and salt.

VANILLA GLAZE

Mix 2 cups powdered sugar, ¼ cup margarine or butter, softened, 1½ teaspoons vanilla and 2 tablespoons hot water. Stir in 1 to 2 teaspoons additional hot water until smooth and of desired consistency.

Molasses-Fruit Bars

½ cup sugar
½ cup molasses
¼ cup shortening
1 egg
½ cup milk
2 cups all-purpose flour*
1½ teaspoons baking powder
½ teaspoon salt
¼ teaspoon baking soda
1½ cups raisins or cut-up dates
1 cup chopped nuts

Heat oven to 350°. Mix sugar, molasses, shortening and egg. Stir in remaining ingredients. Spread in greased baking pan, 13x9x2 inches. Bake until set, about 25 minutes; cool. Frost with Orange-Lemon Frosting (page 16) or sprinkle with powdered sugar if desired. Cut into bars, 3x1 inch.   ABOUT 3 DOZEN.

*If using self-rising flour, omit baking powder and salt.

Granola-Plum Bars

1 cup packed brown sugar
½ cup margarine or butter, softened
¼ cup shortening
2 cups granola
1¾ cups all-purpose flour
1 teaspoon salt
1 jar (12 ounces) plum preserves

Heat oven to 400°. Mix brown sugar, margarine and shortening. Stir in granola, flour and salt. Press half of the granola mixture in greased baking pan, 13x9x2 inches. Spread with preserves; top with remaining granola mixture, pressing lightly. Bake until light brown, 25 to 30 minutes. Cut into bars, 2x1 inch, while warm. 4 DOZEN.

Granola-Date Bars: Omit plum preserves. Mix 1 package (16 ounces) dates, cut up (about 3 cups), 1½ cups water and ¼ cup sugar in saucepan. Cook over low heat, stirring constantly, until thickened, about 10 minutes. Spread over granola mixture in pan. Top with remaining granola mixture.

Granola-Sunflower Nut Bars

¼ cup margarine or butter
3 cups granola
¾ cup toasted salted sunflower nuts
1 can (14 ounces) sweetened condensed milk

Heat oven to 325°. Heat margarine in baking pan, 13x9x2 inches, in oven until melted. Rotate pan until margarine covers bottom. Sprinkle with granola. Bake 15 minutes.

Sprinkle sunflower nuts over granola; pour milk over sunflower nuts. Bake until golden brown, about 20 minutes. Loosen edges from sides of pan while warm; cool. Cut into bars, 2x1 inch. 4 DOZEN.

Pumpkin Bars

Pictured on page 17.

2 cups sugar
½ cup vegetable oil
1 can (16 ounces) pumpkin
4 eggs, beaten
2 cups buttermilk baking mix
2 teaspoons ground cinnamon
½ cup raisins
   Cream Cheese Frosting (below)

Heat oven to 350°. Beat sugar, oil, pumpkin and eggs in large mixer bowl on medium speed, scraping bowl occasionally, 1 minute. Stir in baking mix, cinnamon and raisins. Pour into greased jelly roll pan, 15½x10½x1 inch. Bake until wooden pick inserted in center comes out clean, 25 to 30 minutes; cool. Frost with Cream Cheese Frosting. Cut into bars, 2x1 inch. Store in refrigerator.   ABOUT 5 DOZEN.

CREAM CHEESE FROSTING
1 package (3 ounces) cream cheese, softened
⅓ cup margarine or butter, softened
1 tablespoon milk
1 teaspoon vanilla
2 cups powdered sugar

Beat cream cheese, margarine, milk and vanilla until creamy. Stir in powdered sugar until smooth and of desired consistency.

Mincemeat-Granola Squares

½ cup packed brown sugar
⅓ cup margarine or butter, softened
1 cup granola, slightly crushed
½ cup all-purpose flour
¼ teaspoon salt
1 cup prepared mincemeat
   Glaze (below)

Heat oven to 400°. Mix brown sugar and margarine. Stir in granola, flour and salt; press in greased baking pan, 9x9x2 inches. Spread with mincemeat. Bake until edges are golden brown, 20 to 25 minutes; cool. Drizzle with Glaze. Cut into 2-inch squares.   ABOUT 1½ DOZEN.

GLAZE
Beat ½ cup powdered sugar, ¼ teaspoon vanilla and about 2½ teaspoons water until smooth and of desired consistency.

Spicy Raisin Bars

2 cups raisins
1¼ cups water
1 cup packed brown sugar
⅓ cup shortening
2 cups all-purpose flour*
2 teaspoons ground cinnamon
1 teaspoon salt
1 teaspoon baking soda
1 teaspoon baking powder
½ teaspoon ground nutmeg
½ teaspoon ground cloves
½ cup chopped nuts, if desired
   Powdered sugar

Heat oven to 350°. Mix raisins, water, brown sugar and shortening in saucepan. Heat to boiling, stirring constantly; remove from heat and cool.

Mix flour, cinnamon, salt, baking soda, baking powder, nutmeg and cloves; stir into raisin mixture. Mix in nuts. Spread in greased baking pan, 13x9x2 inches. Bake until top springs back when touched, 35 to 40 minutes; cool. Sprinkle with powdered sugar. Cut into bars, 3x1 inch. Store in airtight container.   ABOUT 3 DOZEN.

*If using self-rising flour, omit salt, baking soda and baking powder.

Frosted Fruit Bars

1 cup sugar
⅓ cup shortening
⅓ cup margarine or butter, softened
1 egg
1 tablespoon grated orange peel, if desired
¼ cup orange or pineapple juice
2½ cups all-purpose flour
1 teaspoon baking soda
½ teaspoon salt
½ teaspoon ground cinnamon
½ teaspoon ground nutmeg
1 cup raisins
1 cup mixed candied fruit
   Powdered Sugar Glaze (below)

Heat oven to 400°. Mix sugar, shortening, margarine, egg, orange peel and orange juice. Stir in remaining ingredients except glaze. Spread in greased jelly roll pan, 15½x10½x1 inch. Bake until top springs back when touched, about 15 minutes; cool slightly. Spread with Powdered Sugar Glaze. Cut into bars, 3x2 inches. ABOUT 2 DOZEN.

POWDERED SUGAR GLAZE
Beat 1½ cups powdered sugar, ¼ teaspoon vanilla and 2 to 3 tablespoons milk until smooth and of desired consistency.

Chewy Fruitcake Bars

2 cups buttermilk baking mix
2 tablespoons sugar
¼ cup firm margarine or butter
1 cup flaked coconut
2 cups cut-up mixed candied fruit
1 cup snipped dates, if desired
1 cup chopped nuts
1 can (14 ounces) sweetened condensed milk

Heat oven to 350°. Mix baking mix and sugar; cut in margarine thoroughly. Press in ungreased jelly roll pan, 15½x10½x1 inch, with floured hands. Bake 10 minutes.

Sprinkle coconut over baked layer. Layer candied fruit and dates over coconut. Sprinkle with nuts. Drizzle milk over top. Bake until light golden brown, 25 to 30 minutes; cool. Cut into bars, 2x1 inch.   ABOUT 5 DOZEN.

Spumoni Bars

½ cup powdered sugar
½ cup shortening
2 eggs, separated
1 cup all-purpose flour*
½ cup ground almonds, if desired
1 can (14 ounces) sweetened condensed
      milk
¼ cup lemon juice
1 teaspoon vanilla
½ cup chopped maraschino cherries,
      drained
½ cup granulated sugar
½ cup roasted diced almonds

Heat oven to 350°. Beat powdered sugar, shortening and egg yolks until blended. Stir in flour and ground almonds. Press in ungreased baking pan, 13x9x2 inches. Bake 15 minutes.

Beat milk, lemon juice and vanilla. Stir in cherries. Beat egg whites in small mixer bowl until foamy. Beat in granulated sugar, 1 table-spoon at a time; continue beating until stiff and glossy. Do not underbeat. Spread cherry mixture over baked layer. Carefully spread meringue over cherry mixture; sprinkle with diced almonds. Bake 20 minutes. Cut into bars, 2x1 inch, while warm. Store in refrigerator. 4 DOZEN.

*Self-rising flour can be used in this recipe.

Holiday Nut Bars

1 cup half-and-half
⅔ cup shortening
½ cup sugar
2 eggs, separated
1 tablespoon sherry flavoring
¼ teaspoon almond extract
1¾ cups all-purpose flour*
2 teaspoons baking powder
1 teaspoon salt
½ cup flaked coconut
½ cup chopped blanched almonds
¼ cup chopped pecans
¼ cup cut-up citron
      Easy Frosting (below)

Heat oven to 400°. Mix half-and-half, shortening, sugar, egg yolks, sherry flavoring and almond extract. Stir in remaining ingredients except egg whites and frosting. Beat egg whites until stiff but not dry; fold into flour mixture. Spread in greased baking pan, 13x9x2 inches. Bake until light brown, about 25 minutes. Frost with Easy Frosting while warm; cool. Cut into bars, 3x1 inch.   ABOUT 3 DOZEN.

*If using self-rising flour, omit baking powder and salt.

EASY FROSTING
Beat 1 cup powdered sugar, ¼ teaspoon salt, ½ teaspoon vanilla and 1 tablespoon plus 1½ teaspoons milk or 1 tablespoon water until smooth and of spreading consistency.

Rolled Cookies

Sugar Cookies

1½ cups powdered sugar
  1 cup margarine or butter, softened
  1 egg
  1 teaspoon vanilla
  ½ teaspoon almond extract
2½ cups all-purpose* or whole wheat flour
  1 teaspoon baking soda
  1 teaspoon cream of tartar
     Granulated sugar

Mix powdered sugar, margarine, egg, vanilla and almond extract. Stir in flour, baking soda and cream of tartar. Cover and refrigerate at least 3 hours.

Heat oven to 375°. Divide dough into halves. Roll each half 3/16 inch thick on lightly floured cloth-covered board. Cut into desired shapes with 2- to 2½-inch cookie cutters; sprinkle with granulated sugar. Place on lightly greased cookie sheet. Bake until edges are light brown, 7 to 8 minutes.   ABOUT 5 DOZEN.

*If using self-rising flour, omit baking soda and cream of tartar.

Confetti Balloons: Divide dough into 3 equal parts. Tint each part with red, green or yellow food color. Cover each part and refrigerate at least 3 hours. Heat oven to 375°. Roll dough 3/16 inch thick. Cut into 2- or 3-inch rounds. Sprinkle with colored sugars. Bake on lightly greased cookie sheet 7 to 8 minutes. Arrange some cookies on pieces of string to resemble clusters of balloons.   ABOUT 5 DOZEN.

Color Wheel Cookies: Divide dough into halves; divide 1 half into 4 equal parts. Tint each of the 4 parts with different food color. Cover each part and refrigerate at least 3 hours. Heat oven to 375°. Roll dough 1/16 inch thick. Cut plain dough into 2½-inch rounds. Place on lightly greased cookie sheet. Cut colored doughs into 2½-inch rounds. Cut each of the colored rounds into quarters. Place 1 quarter of each color on plain rounds. Bake 6 to 10 minutes.   ABOUT 2½ DOZEN.

Cookie Puppets: After refrigerating, roll dough ¼ inch thick. Cut with patterns traced from storybooks or with cookie cutters. Press lightly onto wooden skewers. Bake as directed and decorate as desired.   ABOUT 2 DOZEN.

Stained Glass Cookies: Divide dough into halves. Tint portions of 1 half of the dough with about 5 different food colors. Cover each part and refrigerate at least 3 hours. Heat oven to 375°. Roll plain dough 1/8 inch thick on lightly floured cloth-covered board. Cut with tree, star, ball and other decorative cookie cutters. Place on lightly greased cookie sheet. Roll colored doughs 1/8 inch thick; cut out different shapes to fit on each plain cookie shape. Bake until golden, 7 to 8 minutes.

Snowflake Cookies

1 cup sugar
¾ cup shortening (part margarine or
   butter, softened)
2 eggs
1 teaspoon vanilla or ½ teaspoon
   lemon extract
2½ cups all-purpose flour *
1 teaspoon baking powder
1 teaspoon salt
1 container (16.5 ounces) vanilla ready-to-
   spread frosting

Mix sugar, shortening, eggs and vanilla. Stir in flour, baking powder and salt. Cover and refrigerate at least 1 hour.

Heat oven to 400°. Roll dough ⅛ inch thick on lightly floured cloth-covered board. Cut into 2½-inch star shapes. Place on ungreased cookie sheet. Bake until light brown, 6 to 8 minutes. Remove from cookie sheet; cool. Put cookies together in pairs with about ¼ teaspoon frosting (do not match points of stars). Heat remaining frosting over low heat until thin. Tint with food color if desired. Pour about 1 teaspoon frosting over each pair of stars.   ABOUT 2 DOZEN.

*Do not use self-rising flour in this recipe.

Paintbrush Cookies

Pictured at right.

Prepare dough as directed for Sugar Cookies (page 25) or Snowflake Cookies (above). After rolling out dough, cut into desired shapes with cookie cutters. Cut no more than 12 cookies at a time to keep them from drying out.

Prepare Egg Yolk Paint (below). Paint designs (flowers, plaids, stripes—be creative) on cookies with small paintbrushes. Bake as directed in recipe.

EGG YOLK PAINT
Mix 1 egg yolk and ¼ teaspoon water. Divide mixture among several small custard cups. Tint each with different food color to make bright colors. If paint thickens while standing, stir in few drops water.

Stop-and-Go Cookies

Pictured at right.

Prepare dough as directed for Snowflake Cookies (left) except—decrease vanilla to ½ teaspoon. After refrigerating, heat oven to 400°. Roll dough ¼ inch thick on lightly floured cloth-covered board. Cut into rectangles, 3x2 inches, or 3-inch rounds. Make 3 indentations in each cookie with handle of wooden spoon. Place on ungreased cookie sheet. Bake until light brown, 6 to 8 minutes; cool. Fill indentations with strawberry preserves, orange marmalade and mint-flavored apple jelly to resemble traffic lights.   2½ TO 3 DOZEN.

Blue Jeans

Prepare dough as directed for Snowflake Cookies (left). After refrigerating, heat oven to 400°. Roll dough ⅛ inch thick on lightly floured cloth-covered board. Cut into blue jeans shapes. Place on ungreased cookie sheet. Cut pockets from remaining dough; place on blue jeans. Bake until light brown, 6 to 8 minutes; cool. Frost with Frosting (below); let stand until completely dry. Decorate with Trim (below), using decorators' tube with number 2 writing tip.   ABOUT 1½ DOZEN.

FROSTING
Beat 1½ cups powdered sugar, scant ¼ teaspoon blue food color and 3 to 4 tablespoons milk until smooth and of spreading consistency.

TRIM
Beat ½ cup powdered sugar and 3 to 4 teaspoons milk until smooth and of desired consistency.

Cookies children love—Hand Cookies (page 34), Stop-and-Go Cookies (page 26), Paintbrush Cookies (page 26) and Quick Peanut Butter Stars (page 81)

To pack cookies for mailing, wrap in pairs back to back, like these Jumbo Molasses Cookies (page 44).

For extra cushioning, you may want to tuck only one end of wrap under; fold the other end over the top.

Pack cookie pairs as close together as possible; then pad with crushed paper. See page 5 for more packing tips.

Fried cookies—Rosettes (page 92)

Light Ginger Cookies (page 31) shaped like doves decorate this homemade wreath.

Holiday Cutouts

Prepare dough as directed for Sugar Cookies (page 25), Snowflake Cookies (page 26) or Honey-Lemon Cookies (page 43). After rolling out dough, cut into assorted shapes (below) with cookie cutters or cut with patterns traced from storybooks. (To hang cookies on Christmas tree, loop a piece of green string and press ends into underside of each cookie before baking.) Bake as directed in recipe. Decorate as suggested with Creamy Frosting (below).

CREAMY FROSTING
1 cup powdered sugar
½ teaspoon vanilla
¼ teaspoon salt
 About 1 tablespoon water or 1 to 2
  tablespoons half-and-half
 Assorted food colors

Mix powdered sugar, vanilla and salt. Beat in water until smooth and of spreading consistency. Tint parts of frosting with food colors as directed. (Use liquid food color for light colors, paste food color for deeper colors. Paste food color is available through mail-order baking equipment stores.)

Angels: Spread plain frosting over robe and face; spread wings with light blue frosting.

Christmas Trees: Spread with plain frosting and sprinkle with green sugar. Decorate with tiny colored candies.

Santa Clauses: Outline with red frosting. Decorate bag with tiny colored candies and spread boots with melted chocolate.

Stockings: Sprinkle colored sugar on heels and toes before baking or outline heels and toes with tinted frosting after baking.

Wreaths: Spread with plain frosting and sprinkle with green sugar. Decorate with clusters of berries made from red frosting and leaves made from green frosting.

Light Ginger Cookies

When cut into your favorite Christmas-cookie shapes, these cookies can be used to make a unique Christmas wreath. *Pictured at left.*

1 cup powdered sugar
1 cup margarine or butter, softened
1 tablespoon vinegar
2¼ cups all-purpose flour *
1½ to 2 teaspoons ground ginger
¾ teaspoon baking soda
¼ teaspoon salt

Heat oven to 400°. Mix powdered sugar, margarine and vinegar. Stir in remaining ingredients. (If dough is too dry, work in milk or cream, 1 teaspoon at a time.) Roll ⅛ inch thick on lightly floured cloth-covered board. Cut into desired shapes with cookie cutters. Place on ungreased cookie sheet. Bake until light brown, 6 to 8 minutes. Cool slightly; carefully remove from cookie sheet. Decorate with Decorators' Frosting (below) if desired.   ABOUT 4 DOZEN.

*Do not use self-rising flour in this recipe.

Note: Using a drinking straw, poke a hole in the top of each cookie before baking. Attach to wreath with wire or tie on with ribbon.

DECORATORS' FROSTING
Beat 2 cups powdered sugar, ½ teaspoon vanilla and about 2 tablespoons half-and-half until smooth and of spreading consistency. Frosting can be tinted with food color and used in decorators' tube if desired.

Bear Claws

½ cup granulated sugar
¼ cup margarine or butter, softened
2 tablespoons shortening
1 egg
1 teaspoon vanilla
1¼ cups all-purpose flour*
½ teaspoon baking powder
½ teaspoon salt
About 3 tablespoons raspberry jam
About 3 tablespoons chopped nuts
About 3 tablespoons powdered sugar

Mix granulated sugar, margarine, shortening, egg and vanilla. Stir in flour, baking powder and salt. Cover and refrigerate at least 1 hour.

Heat oven to 400°. Roll dough into 12-inch square on lightly floured cloth-covered board. Cut into 3-inch squares. Spread about ½ teaspoon jam down center of each square; sprinkle with about ½ teaspoon nuts. Fold 1 edge of dough over filling; fold other edge over top. Place on greased cookie sheet. Make 4 or 5 cuts in 1 long side of each cookie; spread cuts slightly apart. Sprinkle each cookie with about ½ teaspoon powdered sugar. Bake until light brown, about 6 minutes.   ABOUT 1½ DOZEN.

*Do not use self-rising flour in this recipe.

Pinwheels: Cut unfolded 3-inch squares diagonally from each corner almost to center. Fold every other point to center to make pinwheel. Spoon ½ teaspoon jam onto center of each pinwheel; sprinkle with ½ teaspoon nuts and ½ teaspoon powdered sugar. Bake as directed.

Lollipops: Drop dough by teaspoonfuls onto ungreased cookie sheet; flatten slightly. Place 1 wooden ice-cream stick and 1 milk chocolate star on each circle. Top with another teaspoonful dough; press together. Bake until light brown, about 8 minutes.

Mexican Cookies: Substitute anise extract for the vanilla. Cut 12-inch square into 3-inch flower shapes with cookie cutter; sprinkle with colored sugar. Bake as directed.

Honey-Molasses Cookies

Bake these traditional German *Lebkuchen*, or honey cakes, several weeks ahead to give them time to mellow.

½ cup honey
½ cup molasses
¾ cup packed brown sugar
1 egg
1 teaspoon grated lemon peel
1 tablespoon lemon juice
2¾ cups all-purpose flour*
1 teaspoon ground allspice
1 teaspoon ground cloves
1 teaspoon ground nutmeg
1 teaspoon ground cinnamon
½ teaspoon baking soda
⅓ cup cut-up citron
⅓ cup chopped nuts
Cookie Glaze (below)

Mix honey and molasses in saucepan. Heat to boiling; remove from heat. Cool completely. Stir in brown sugar, egg, lemon peel and lemon juice. Mix in remaining ingredients except Cookie Glaze. Cover and refrigerate at least 8 hours.

Heat oven to 400°. Roll small amount of dough at a time ¼ inch thick on lightly floured cloth-covered board (keep remaining dough refrigerated). Cut into rectangles, 2½x1½ inches. Place about 1 inch apart on greased cookie sheet. Bake until no indentation remains when touched, 10 to 12 minutes. Brush glaze over cookies. Immediately remove from cookie sheet; cool. Store in airtight container.   ABOUT 5 DOZEN.

*Do not use self-rising flour in this recipe.

COOKIE GLAZE

Mix 1 cup sugar and ½ cup water in saucepan. Cook over medium heat to 230° or just until small amount of mixture spins 2-inch thread; remove from heat. Stir in ¼ cup powdered sugar. (If glaze becomes sugary while brushing cookies, heat slightly, adding a little water, until clear again.)

Heart Cookies

Pictured on page 69.

Prepare dough as directed for Sugar Cookies (page 25) except—substitute mint flavoring for the almond extract. After refrigerating, heat oven to 375°. Roll dough ¼ inch thick. Cut into 3½-inch heart shapes. Paint Valentine's Day messages on cookies with Artist's Coloring or Cookie Paint (below). Place on ungreased cookie sheet. Bake until golden, 8 to 10 minutes.   2 TO 2½ DOZEN.

ARTIST'S COLORING
Beat 1 egg white until foamy. Beat in 1 cup powdered sugar until smooth. Divide among custard cups. Tint each with about 4 drops food color.

COOKIE PAINT
Tint small amounts evaporated milk with different food colors.

Easter Egg Cookies

Pictured on page 69.

Prepare dough as directed for Sugar Cookies (page 25). After refrigerating, roll dough ⅛ inch thick. Cut with egg shaped cutter made by bending and shaping round cookie cutter. Bake as directed and decorate with Easy Creamy Frosting (page 41).

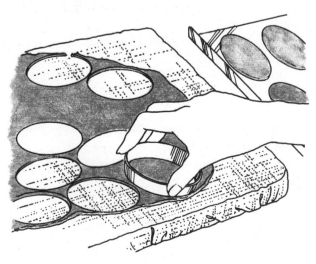

Hamantaschen

These filled three-cornered cookies are served at the joyous Jewish festival of Purim. *Pictured on page 69.*

1	**cup sugar**
⅓	**cup vegetable oil**
3	**eggs**
	Grated peel and juice from 1 orange
3¼	**cups all-purpose flour**
2	**teaspoons baking powder**
½	**teaspoon salt**
	Filling (below)

Beat sugar, oil and eggs until blended. Stir in orange peel and orange juice. Mix in flour, baking powder and salt. Cover and refrigerate at least 2 hours.

Heat oven to 375°. Divide dough into halves. Roll each half ⅛ inch thick on lightly floured cloth-covered board. Cut into 3-inch rounds. Spoon 1 teaspoon Filling onto each round. Fold each round to form triangle. Pinch edges together to form slight ridge. Place on lightly greased cookie sheet. Bake until golden brown, 12 to 15 minutes.   ABOUT 4½ DOZEN.

FILLING
Mix 1 pound cut-up cooked prunes, 1 cup chopped nuts, 1 tablespoon sugar and 1 tablespoon lemon juice.

Quick Chocolate Wafers

1	**package (11 ounces) pie crust sticks or mix**
1	**ounce melted unsweetened chocolate (cool)**
1	**cup powdered sugar**
½	**cup chopped nuts**
½	**teaspoon vanilla**
¼	**cup water**

Mix all ingredients. Cover and refrigerate at least 1 hour.

Heat oven to 375°. Roll dough ⅛ inch thick on lightly floured cloth-covered board. Cut into 2-inch rounds. Place on ungreased cookie sheet. Bake 10 minutes. Cool slightly; remove from cookie sheet.   ABOUT 3 DOZEN.

Sour Cream Cookies

Looking for a cookie that's a conversation piece? Try the Hand Cookies variation. *Pictured on page 27.*

  1 **cup sugar**
 ¼ **cup margarine or butter, softened**
 ¼ **cup shortening**
  1 **egg**
  1 **teaspoon vanilla**
2⅔ **cups all-purpose flour** *
  1 **teaspoon baking powder**
 ½ **teaspoon baking soda**
 ½ **teaspoon salt**
 ¼ **teaspoon ground nutmeg**
 ½ **cup dairy sour cream**
     Decorators' Frosting (below)

Heat oven to 425°. Mix 1 cup sugar, the margarine, shortening, egg and vanilla. Stir in remaining ingredients except frosting. Divide dough into 3 equal parts. Roll each part ¼ inch thick on lightly floured cloth-covered board. Cut into desired shapes with 2-inch cookie cutter; pipe with Decorators' Frosting. Place about 1 inch apart on ungreased cookie sheet. Bake until no indentation remains when touched, 6 to 8 minutes.   4 TO 5 DOZEN.

*If using self-rising flour, omit baking powder, baking soda and salt.

DECORATORS' FROSTING

Mix 2 cups powdered sugar and 2 to 3 tablespoons water until frosting is of a consistency that can be used easily in a decorators' tube or envelope cone (below) and yet hold its shape. To make an envelope cone, place about ⅓ cup frosting in the corner of an envelope; fold sides toward center. Snip off corner to make tip.

Chocolate Sour Cream Cookies: Mix 1 ounce melted unsweetened chocolate (cool) into 1 part dough.

Coconut Sour Cream Cookies: Mix ¼ cup cookie coconut into 1 part dough.

Hand Cookies: Use the basic dough or any of the flavored variations. After rolling, trace around hand with knife or pastry wheel. Cut remaining dough into desired shapes.   ABOUT 6 HAND COOKIES AND 1 DOZEN 2-INCH COOKIES.

Molded Sour Cream Cookies: Shape dough by tablespoonfuls into balls. Flatten on cookie sheet with greased bottom of glass dipped in sugar.

Orange Sour Cream Cookies: Mix 1 tablespoon grated orange peel into 1 part dough.

Peanut Butter Sour Cream Cookies: Mix 1 tablespoon creamy peanut butter into 1 part dough.

Cream Wafers

2 **cups all-purpose flour** *
1 **cup margarine or butter, softened**
⅓ **cup whipping cream**
   Sugar
   Filling (below)

Mix flour, margarine and cream. Cover and refrigerate.

Heat oven to 375°. Roll about ⅓ of the dough at a time ⅛ inch thick on floured cloth-covered board (keep remaining dough refrigerated). Cut into 1½-inch rounds. Coat both sides with sugar. Place on ungreased cookie sheet. Prick each round with fork about 4 times. Bake just until set but not brown, 7 to 9 minutes. Remove from cookie sheet; cool. Put cookies together in pairs with Filling.   ABOUT 5 DOZEN.

*Self-rising flour can be used in this recipe.

FILLING

Mix ¾ cup powdered sugar, ¼ cup margarine or butter, softened, and 1 teaspoon vanilla until smooth and fluffy. Beat in few drops water, if necessary, until smooth and of spreading consistency. Tint parts of filling with few drops different food colors.

Fancy Bonbon Cookies

1 cup sugar
⅔ cup margarine or butter, softened
1 package (3 ounces) cream cheese, softened
1 egg
1 teaspoon finely grated lemon peel
½ teaspoon lemon juice
2 cups all-purpose flour*
½ teaspoon baking powder
½ teaspoon salt
⅛ teaspoon baking soda
   Orange marmalade
   Pastel Frosting (below)

Mix sugar, margarine, cream cheese, egg, lemon peel and lemon juice until light and fluffy. Stir in flour, baking powder, salt and baking soda. Cover and refrigerate at least 3 hours.

Heat oven to 350°. Roll ¼ of the dough at a time ⅛ inch thick on lightly floured board (keep remaining dough refrigerated). Cut into 1-inch rounds. Place half of the rounds on lightly greased cookie sheet. Spoon about ¼ teaspoon marmalade onto center of each round; top with remaining rounds. Pinch edges with floured hands to seal. Bake until edges are light brown, 8 to 10 minutes; cool. Frost raised centers with Pastel Frosting. ABOUT 7 DOZEN.

*Do not use self-rising flour in this recipe.

PASTEL FROSTING
Beat 3 cups powdered sugar, ¾ teaspoon salt, 1½ teaspoons vanilla and 3 tablespoons water or ¼ cup cream until smooth and of spreading consistency. Divide frosting among small bowls. Tint each with different food color.

Cream Cookies

2 eggs
1 cup sugar
1 cup whipping cream
3¾ cups all-purpose flour*
3 teaspoons baking powder
1 teaspoon salt
   Frosting (below)

Beat eggs in large bowl until foamy. Beat in sugar gradually. Stir in cream. Mix in flour, baking powder and salt. Cover and refrigerate at least 1 hour.

Heat oven to 375°. Roll dough ¼ to ⅜ inch thick on floured cloth-covered board. Cut into 2-inch squares. Make 2 cuts, ½ inch long, on each side of each square, not cutting all the way through. Place on greased cookie sheet. Bake until edges are light brown, 10 to 13 minutes; cool. Frost with Frosting. ABOUT 4 DOZEN.

*If using self-rising flour, omit baking powder and salt.

FROSTING
Beat 1 cup powdered sugar, 1 tablespoon margarine or butter, softened, ½ teaspoon vanilla and 1 tablespoon plus 1 teaspoon milk until smooth and of spreading consistency. Stir in additional milk if necessary. Divide frosting into halves. Tint each half with few drops different food color.

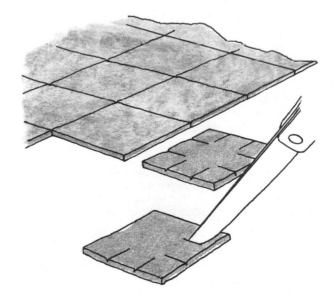

Malted Milk Rounds

2 cups packed brown sugar
1 cup margarine or butter, softened
⅓ cup dairy sour cream
2 eggs
2 teaspoons vanilla
4 cups all-purpose flour*
¾ cup malted milk powder (plain)
2 teaspoons baking powder
½ teaspoon baking soda
½ teaspoon salt
   Malted Milk Frosting (below)

Heat oven to 375°. Mix brown sugar, margarine, sour cream, eggs and vanilla. Stir in flour, malted milk powder, baking powder, baking soda and salt. Roll ¼ inch thick on floured board. Cut into 2½-inch rounds. Place on ungreased cookie sheet. Bake until no indentation remains when touched, 10 to 11 minutes; cool. Frost with Malted Milk Frosting. ABOUT 5 DOZEN.

*If using self-rising flour, omit baking soda and salt.

MALTED MILK FROSTING
½ cup packed brown sugar
¼ cup margarine or butter
¼ cup milk or cream
3¾ cups powdered sugar
⅓ cup malted milk powder (plain)
½ teaspoon vanilla

Cook brown sugar, margarine and milk over medium heat until margarine is melted; remove from heat. Stir in remaining ingredients.

Scotch Shortbread

¾ cup margarine or butter, softened
¼ cup sugar
2 cups all-purpose flour*

Heat oven to 350°. Mix margarine and sugar. Work in flour with hands. (If dough is crumbly, mix in 1 to 2 tablespoons margarine or butter, softened.) Roll ½ to ⅓ inch thick on lightly floured cloth-covered board. Cut into small shapes (leaves, ovals, squares, triangles, etc.). Place ½ inch apart on ungreased cookie sheet. Bake until set, about 20 minutes. Immediately remove from cookie sheet. ABOUT 2 DOZEN.

*Do not use self-rising flour in this recipe.

Oatmeal Shortbread

1 cup margarine or butter, softened
½ cup packed brown sugar
1 teaspoon vanilla
1 cup all-purpose flour*
½ teaspoon baking soda
2 cups oats

Mix margarine, brown sugar and vanilla. Stir in remaining ingredients. Cover and refrigerate at least 2 hours.

Heat oven to 350°. Roll dough ¼ inch thick on lightly floured board. Cut into 1½-inch squares or desired shapes. Place on ungreased cookie sheet. Bake 10 to 12 minutes. 3½ TO 4 DOZEN.

*Do not use self-rising flour in this recipe.

Almond-Cherry Strips

Pictured on page 67.

2½ cups all-purpose flour
1 cup sugar
½ cup whipping cream
¼ cup margarine or butter, softened
1 egg, separated
2 teaspoons baking powder
1 teaspoon almond extract
½ teaspoon salt
1¾ cups powdered sugar
½ teaspoon almond extract
¼ cup chopped almonds
¼ cup cut-up red candied cherries

Mix flour, sugar, whipping cream, margarine, egg yolk, baking powder, 1 teaspoon almond extract and the salt. Work with hands until blended. Cover and refrigerate at least 1 hour.

Heat oven to 375°. Divide dough into halves. Roll each half into rectangle, 8x6 inches, on well-floured cloth-covered board. Square off rounded corners. Place on greased cookie sheet.

Beat egg white until foamy. Beat in powdered sugar gradually; continue beating until stiff and glossy. Do not underbeat. Beat in ½ teaspoon almond extract. Spread egg white over dough; arrange almonds and cherries on top. Cut into strips, about 2x1 inch. Bake until edges are light brown, about 10 minutes. ABOUT 4 DOZEN.

Rich Cookie Strips

In Sweden these cookies are called *Finska Kakor,* or Finnish Cakes.

¾　cup margarine or butter, softened
¼　cup sugar
　1　teaspoon almond extract
　2　cups all-purpose flour*
　1　egg white, slightly beaten
　1　tablespoon sugar
⅓　cup finely chopped blanched almonds

Mix margarine, ¼ cup sugar and the almond extract. Work in flour with hands. Cover and refrigerate.

Heat oven to 350°. Roll dough ¼ inch thick. Cut into strips, 2½x¾ inch; brush with egg white. Mix 1 tablespoon sugar and the almonds; sprinkle over strips. Carefully transfer several at a time to ungreased cookie sheet, separating cookies slightly. Bake until very delicate brown, 17 to 20 minutes.　ABOUT 4 DOZEN.

*Do not use self-rising flour in this recipe.

Almond Cookies

　2　cups sugar
　1　cup margarine or butter, softened
　1　cup shortening
　2　teaspoons almond extract
　1　teaspoon vanilla
　1　egg
3½　cups all-purpose flour*
　1　teaspoon baking powder
　1　package (3 ounces) whole blanched
　　　almonds

Heat oven to 375°. Mix sugar, margarine, shortening, almond extract, vanilla and egg. Stir in flour and baking powder. Roll ¼ inch thick on floured board. Cut into 2-inch rounds. Place almond in center of each cookie. Place on ungreased cookie sheet. Bake until edges are light brown, 10 to 11 minutes. Cool 1 minute; remove from cookie sheet.　ABOUT 5½ DOZEN.

*If using self-rising flour, omit baking powder.

Sesame Seed Cookies

These bowknot cookies are traditional for holidays in the Sparta region of Greece.

⅔　cup sesame seed
1¾　cups sugar
　1　cup margarine or butter, softened
　2　eggs
　4　cups all-purpose flour*
　2　teaspoons baking powder
½　teaspoon salt
¼　cup water

Heat sesame seed over medium heat, stirring frequently, until light brown; remove from heat. Mix sugar, margarine and eggs until fluffy. Stir in ⅓ cup of the sesame seed. Mix flour, baking powder and salt. Stir flour mixture and water alternately into sugar mixture. Cover and refrigerate at least 2 hours.

Heat oven to 350°. Roll dough ⅛ inch thick on lightly floured board. Cut into strips, 2½x¾ inch. Coat 1 side of each strip with remaining sesame seed. Fold 1 end over at right angle to other end, to resemble bowknot. Place on ungreased cookie sheet. Bake until light brown, 8 to 10 minutes.　ABOUT 9 DOZEN.

*If using self-rising flour, omit baking powder and salt.

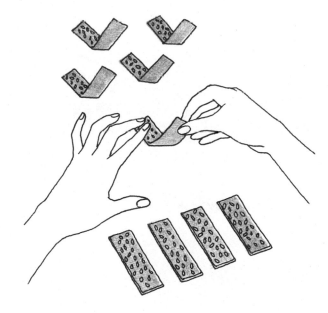

Peanut Butter Sticks

½ cup granulated sugar
½ cup packed brown sugar
½ cup crunchy peanut butter
½ cup margarine or butter, softened
¼ cup shortening
1 egg
1¼ cups all-purpose flour*
¾ teaspoon baking soda
½ teaspoon baking powder
¼ teaspoon salt
About ½ cup strawberry preserves
Peanut Butter Glaze (below)

Mix sugars, peanut butter, margarine, shortening and egg. Stir in flour, baking soda, baking powder and salt. Cover and refrigerate at least 1 hour.

Heat oven to 375°. Roll dough ¼ inch thick on lightly floured cloth-covered board. Cut into rectangles, 6x1½ inches. Make indentation down center of each with handle of wooden spoon; fill with about 2 teaspoons preserves. Place on ungreased cookie sheet. Bake 8 to 10 minutes. Cool slightly; remove from cookie sheet. Cut cookies diagonally into halves while warm if desired; cool. Drizzle with Peanut Butter Glaze.   ABOUT 14.

*If using self-rising flour, omit baking soda, baking powder and salt.

PEANUT BUTTER GLAZE
Beat 1 cup powdered sugar, 2 tablespoons crunchy peanut butter and 2 to 3 tablespoons water until of desired consistency.

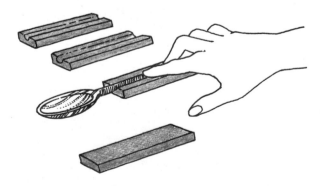

Peanut Butter Cutouts

You can turn these cookies into a child's fantasy come true. *Pictured at right.*

Prepare dough as directed for Peanut Butter Sticks (left) except—substitute creamy peanut butter for the crunchy peanut butter. After refrigerating, heat oven to 375°. Divide dough into halves. Roll each half ⅛ inch thick on lightly floured cloth-covered board. Cut into desired shapes with small cookie cutters. Place on ungreased cookie sheet. Bake 6 to 8 minutes; cool. Frost with Peanut Butter Frosting (below) if desired.   ABOUT 12 DOZEN.

Note: Create new shapes with your cookie cutters—houses, wagons, railroad cars, snowmen, sailboats. Just press the cutout cookies together and bake.

PEANUT BUTTER FROSTING
Beat 3 cups powdered sugar, ¼ cup peanut butter and ¼ to ⅓ cup milk until of spreading consistency. Stir in ½ cup chopped Spanish peanuts.

Pumpkin-shaped Cookies

Pictured on page 69.

Prepare dough as directed for Peanut Butter Sticks (left). After refrigerating, heat oven to 375°. Divide dough into halves. Roll each half ⅛ inch thick on lightly floured cloth-covered board. Cut with pumpkin-shaped cutter or into 3-inch rounds. Place on ungreased cookie sheet. Bake 6 to 8 minutes; cool. Frost generously with Orange Frosting (below); make pumpkin marks with wooden pick. Add stem of green frosting. Outline features with Chocolate Glaze (page 66) or decorate with black gumdrop slices in cat shapes.   ABOUT 4½ DOZEN.

ORANGE FROSTING
Mix 6 cups powdered sugar and ⅔ cup margarine or butter, softened. Beat in about ⅓ cup frozen orange juice concentrate (thawed) until smooth and of spreading consistency. Reserve ⅓ cup of the frosting; tint with green food color. Tint remaining frosting with red and yellow food color to obtain desired shade of orange.

Peanut Butter Cutouts (page 38)—a few cookie cutters, your ingenuity and presto! the circus is in town.

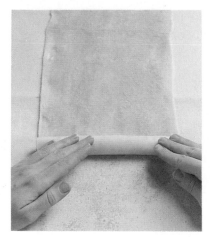

It will be easier to roll rectangle evenly if 7-inch edge is straight.

To seal, pinch roll and rectangle together with dampened fingers.

For easier cutting, be sure to use a thin, sharp knife.

Cinnamon Pinwheel Cookies (page 41)

Peanut Thins

    1   cup packed brown sugar
    ½   cup shortening
    ¼   cup margarine or butter, softened
    ¼   cup peanut butter
    1   egg yolk
    1   teaspoon vanilla
    1¾ cups all-purpose flour*
        Easy Creamy Frosting (right)
    ½   cup chopped peanuts

Heat oven to 350°. Mix brown sugar, shortening, margarine, peanut butter, egg yolk and vanilla. Stir in flour. Divide dough into halves. Roll each half into rectangle, 12x6 inches, on ungreased cookie sheet (be sure edges aren't too thin). Bake until light brown and set, 13 to 14 minutes. Spread with Easy Creamy Frosting while warm; sprinkle with peanuts. Cut into strips, 3x1 inch.   4 DOZEN.

*Self-rising flour can be used in this recipe.

Crisp Ginger Cookies

You can roll these spicy cookies from Moravia paper-thin.

    ⅓   cup molasses
    ¼   cup shortening
    2   tablespoons packed brown sugar
    1¼ cups all-purpose* or whole wheat flour
    ½   teaspoon salt
    ¼   teaspoon baking soda
    ¼   teaspoon baking powder
    ¼   teaspoon ground cinnamon
    ¼   teaspoon ground ginger
    ¼   teaspoon ground cloves
        Dash of ground nutmeg
        Dash of ground allspice
        Easy Creamy Frosting (right)

Mix molasses, shortening and brown sugar. Stir in remaining ingredients except frosting. Cover and refrigerate at least 4 hours.

Heat oven to 375°. Roll dough ⅛ inch thick or paper-thin on floured cloth-covered board. Cut into 3-inch rounds with floured cutter. Place about ½ inch apart on ungreased cookie sheet. Bake until light brown, ⅛-inch-thick cookies about 8 minutes, paper-thin cookies about 5 minutes. Immediately remove from cookie sheet; cool. Frost with Easy Creamy Frosting.   ABOUT 1½ DOZEN OR ABOUT 3 DOZEN.

*If using self-rising flour, omit salt, baking soda and baking powder.

EASY CREAMY FROSTING
Mix 1 cup powdered sugar, ½ teaspoon vanilla and ¼ teaspoon salt. Beat in 1 to 2 tablespoons half-and-half until smooth and of spreading consistency.

Cinnamon Pinwheels

Pictured at left.

    1   cup margarine or butter
    1½ cups all-purpose flour*
    ½   cup dairy sour cream
    3   tablespoons sugar
    1   teaspoon ground cinnamon
    3   tablespoons sugar
    1   tablespoon water

Cut margarine into flour with pastry blender. Stir in sour cream. Cover and refrigerate at least 8 hours.

Mix 3 tablespoons sugar and the cinnamon. Divide dough into halves. Roll 1 half into rectangle, 20x7 inches, on sugared, well-floured cloth-covered board. Sprinkle with half of the sugar-cinnamon mixture. Roll up tightly, beginning at 7-inch side. Roll other half of dough into rectangle, 20x7 inches; sprinkle with remaining sugar-cinnamon mixture. Place loose end of roll on 7-inch side of rectangle; pinch edges to seal. Continue to roll up tightly; pinch edge of dough into roll to seal. Wrap and refrigerate at least 1 hour but no longer than 48 hours.

Heat oven to 350°. Cut roll into ¼-inch slices. Place about 2 inches apart on ungreased cookie sheet. Mix 3 tablespoons sugar and the water; brush over cookies. Bake until golden brown, 20 to 25 minutes.   ABOUT 2 DOZEN.

*Self-rising flour can be used in this recipe. Baking time may be shorter.

Cookie Turnovers

1 cup sugar
½ cup shortening
2 eggs
1 teaspoon vanilla
2½ cups all-purpose flour *
½ teaspoon salt
¼ teaspoon baking soda
   Cherry Filling, Pineapple Filling (below)
      or Fruit Filling (right)
   Milk
   Sugar

Mix 1 cup sugar, the shortening, eggs and vanilla. Stir in flour, salt and baking soda. Cover and refrigerate at least 1 hour. Prepare filling.

Heat oven to 400°. Roll dough 1/16 inch thick on lightly floured cloth-covered board. Cut into 3-inch rounds or squares. Spoon about 1 teaspoon filling onto half of each circle. Fold dough over filling; pinch edges to seal. Place about 1 inch apart on ungreased cookie sheet. Brush with milk; sprinkle with sugar. Bake until very light brown, 8 to 10 minutes. Immediately remove from cookie sheet.   ABOUT 4½ DOZEN.

*If using self-rising flour, omit salt and baking soda.

CHERRY FILLING
¾ cup sugar
3 tablespoons cornstarch
¾ cup orange juice
½ cup maraschino cherry syrup
18 maraschino cherries, chopped
1 tablespoon plus 1½ teaspoons
      margarine or butter

Mix sugar and cornstarch in saucepan. Stir in orange juice gradually. Stir in remaining ingredients. Cook, stirring constantly, until mixture thickens and boils. Boil and stir 1 minute; cool completely.

PINEAPPLE FILLING
1 can (13¼ ounces) crushed pineapple
⅔ cup sugar
3 tablespoons flour
2 tablespoons lemon juice
1 tablespoon margarine or butter
   Dash of ground nutmeg

Drain pineapple thoroughly, reserving ½ cup syrup. Mix sugar and flour in saucepan. Stir in pineapple, reserved pineapple syrup and the remaining ingredients. Cook, stirring constantly, until mixture thickens, about 5 minutes; cool completely.

FRUIT FILLING
2 cups dates, figs or raisins, snipped, or 2
      cups mashed cooked prunes
¾ cup sugar
¾ cup water
½ cup chopped nuts, if desired

Mix all ingredients in saucepan. Cook, stirring constantly, until mixture thickens; cool completely.

Jam Sandwich Cookies

2 cups all-purpose flour *
¾ cup margarine or butter, softened
⅓ cup sugar
½ teaspoon salt
2 eggs
⅓ cup jam
   Vanilla Frosting (below)

Heat oven to 375°. Mix flour, margarine, sugar, salt and eggs. Roll ⅛ inch thick on lightly floured cloth-covered board. Cut into 2-inch rounds. Place on ungreased cookie sheet. Bake until set, 8 to 10 minutes. Remove from cookie sheet; cool. Put cookies together in pairs with jam. Frost with Vanilla Frosting.   ABOUT 3 DOZEN.

*Do not use self-rising flour in this recipe.

VANILLA FROSTING
Mix 1 cup powdered sugar, 1 tablespoon margarine or butter, softened, 1 tablespoon plus 1 teaspoon milk and ¼ teaspoon vanilla. Beat in additional milk, if necessary, until smooth and of spreading consistency.

Gingerbread Boys and Girls

1½ cups dark molasses
1 cup packed brown sugar
⅔ cup cold water
⅓ cup shortening
7 cups all-purpose flour*
2 teaspoons baking soda
2 teaspoons ground ginger
1 teaspoon salt
1 teaspoon ground allspice
1 teaspoon ground cloves
1 teaspoon ground cinnamon
  Frosting (below)

Mix molasses, brown sugar, water and shortening. Stir in remaining ingredients except Frosting. Cover and refrigerate at least 2 hours.

Heat oven to 350°. Roll dough ¼ inch thick on floured board. Cut with floured gingerbread cookie cutter or other favorite cutter. Place about 2 inches apart on lightly greased cookie sheet. Bake until no indentation remains when touched, 10 to 12 minutes; cool. Frost with Frosting.   ABOUT 2½ DOZEN.

*If using self-rising flour, omit baking soda and salt.

FROSTING
Beat 4 cups powdered sugar, 1 teaspoon vanilla and about 5 tablespoons half-and-half until smooth and of spreading consistency. Tint with food color if desired.

Gingerbread Cookies: Decrease flour to 6 cups. Roll dough ½ inch thick. Cut into 2½-inch rounds with floured cookie cutter. Place about 1½ inches apart on lightly greased cookie sheet. Bake about 15 minutes.

Filled Molasses Rounds

½ cup packed brown sugar
½ cup shortening
½ cup molasses
¼ cup buttermilk
1 egg
3 cups all-purpose flour*
1 teaspoon baking soda
1 teaspoon baking powder
1 teaspoon ground cinnamon
½ teaspoon salt
¼ teaspoon ground cloves
¼ teaspoon ground nutmeg
  About ¾ cup orange marmalade
  Cut-up dates, candied fruit or raisins

Heat oven to 375°. Mix brown sugar, shortening, molasses, buttermilk and egg. Stir in flour, baking soda, baking powder, cinnamon, salt, cloves and nutmeg. Divide into 3 equal parts. Roll each part 1/16 inch thick on floured board. Cut into 2-inch rounds. Place half the rounds on ungreased cookie sheet. Spoon about ½ teaspoon marmalade onto center of each; top with remaining rounds. Top each with a piece of date. Bake until no indentation remains when touched, 8 to 9 minutes.   ABOUT 5 DOZEN.

*If using self-rising flour, omit baking soda, baking powder and salt.

Honey-Lemon Cookies

⅓ cup sugar
⅓ cup shortening
⅔ cup honey
1 egg
1 teaspoon lemon extract
2¾ cups all-purpose flour*
1 teaspoon baking soda
1 teaspoon salt

Heat oven to 375°. Mix sugar, shortening, honey, egg and lemon extract. Stir in remaining ingredients. Roll ¼ inch thick. Cut into desired shapes with cookie cutters. Place about 1 inch apart on lightly greased cookie sheet. Bake until no indentation remains when touched, 7 to 8 minutes; cool.   ABOUT 2½ DOZEN.

*If using self-rising flour, decrease baking soda to ¼ teaspoon and omit salt.

Oatmeal-Molasses Cookies

    2 cups all-purpose flour*
    ½ cup packed brown sugar
    ¾ cup shortening
    ¼ cup molasses
    1 egg
    1 teaspoon salt
    ½ teaspoon baking soda
    1 cup oats
       Pumpkin Filling or Date Filling (below)

Heat oven to 375°. Mix flour, brown sugar, shortening, molasses, egg, salt and baking soda. Stir in oats. Roll ⅛ inch thick on lightly floured board. Cut into 2½-inch rounds. Place half of the rounds on ungreased cookie sheet. Spoon about 1 teaspoon Pumpkin Filling onto center of each round. Cut pattern out of each of the remaining rounds. Place cutout rounds on filled rounds; pinch edges to seal. Bake 12 to 15 minutes.   ABOUT 1½ DOZEN.

*If using self-rising flour, omit salt and baking soda.

PUMPKIN FILLING
    1 cup cooked or canned pumpkin
    ½ cup sugar
    ½ teaspoon ground cinnamon
    ½ teaspoon ground ginger
    ¼ teaspoon ground nutmeg

Mix all ingredients.

DATE FILLING
Cook 1 cup cut-up dates, about ½ cup sugar and ¼ cup water, stirring constantly, until thickened. Stir in ½ cup chopped nuts; cool.

Jumbo Molasses Cookies

Pictured on page 28.

    1   cup sugar
    1   cup dark molasses
    ½   cup shortening
    ½   cup water
    4   cups all-purpose flour*
    1½   teaspoons salt
    1½   teaspoons ground ginger
    1   teaspoon baking soda
    ½   teaspoon ground cloves
    ½   teaspoon ground nutmeg
    ¼   teaspoon ground allspice
         Sugar

Mix 1 cup sugar, the molasses, shortening and water. Stir in remaining ingredients except sugar. Cover and refrigerate at least 2 hours.

Heat oven to 375°. Roll dough ¼ inch thick on well-floured cloth-covered board. Cut into 3-inch rounds; sprinkle with sugar. Place about 1½ inches apart on ungreased cookie sheet. Bake until almost no indentation remains when touched, 10 to 12 minutes. Cool 2 minutes; remove from cookie sheet.   ABOUT 3 DOZEN.

*If using self-rising flour, omit salt and baking soda.

Gingerbread Cutouts: Increase flour to 5 cups. Cut dough with floured gingerbread cookie cutter.   ABOUT 2½ DOZEN.

Ice-cream Sandwiches: Cut round bulk ice cream into slices; place each slice between 2 cookies. Freeze at least 1 hour.

Wagon Wheels: Increase flour to 5 cups. Press large raisin onto center of each cookie before baking. If desired, make spoke design radiating from centers of cooled cookies with Decorators' Frosting (page 34).

Whole Wheat Molasses Cookies: Substitute whole wheat flour for the all-purpose flour. It is not necessary to refrigerate dough.

Drop Cookies

Chocolate Drops

Pictured on page 18.

1 cup sugar
½ cup margarine or butter, softened
⅓ cup buttermilk or water
1 egg
2 ounces melted unsweetened chocolate (cool)
1 teaspoon vanilla
1¾ cups all-purpose* or whole wheat flour
½ teaspoon baking soda
½ teaspoon salt
1 cup chopped nuts, if desired
Chocolate Frosting (below) or Browned Butter Frosting (right)

Heat oven to 400°. Mix sugar, margarine, buttermilk, egg, chocolate and vanilla. Stir in flour, baking soda, salt and nuts. Drop by rounded teaspoonfuls about 2 inches apart onto ungreased cookie sheet. Bake until almost no indentation remains when touched, 8 to 10 minutes. Immediately remove from cookie sheet; cool. Frost with Chocolate Frosting. ABOUT 4½ DOZEN.

*If using self-rising flour, omit baking soda and salt.

CHOCOLATE FROSTING
Heat 2 squares (1 ounce each) unsweetened chocolate and 2 tablespoons margarine or butter over low heat until melted; remove from heat. Beat in 3 tablespoons water and about 2 cups powdered sugar until smooth and of spreading consistency.

BROWNED BUTTER FROSTING
Heat ¼ cup butter over low heat until golden brown; remove from heat. Beat in 2 cups powdered sugar, 1 teaspoon vanilla and about 2 tablespoons half-and-half until smooth and of spreading consistency.

Chocolate-Cherry Drops: Substitute 2 cups cut-up candied or maraschino cherries for the nuts. Use Chocolate Frosting.

Chocolate-Peanut Drops: Omit salt. Substitute 2 cups salted peanuts for the nuts. Use Chocolate Frosting.

Cocoa Drops: Increase margarine to ⅔ cup. Omit chocolate and stir in ½ cup cocoa.

Quick Chocolate Chip Drops

⅔ cup packed brown sugar
¼ cup margarine or butter, softened
1 egg
1⅓ cups buttermilk baking mix
¼ cup all-purpose flour
1 package (6 ounces) semisweet chocolate chips

Heat oven to 375°. Mix brown sugar, margarine and egg. Stir in baking mix and flour until smooth. Mix in chocolate chips. Drop by rounded teaspoonfuls about 2 inches apart onto greased cookie sheet. Bake until almost no indentation remains when touched, 8 to 10 minutes. Immediately remove from cookie sheet. ABOUT 2 DOZEN.

Chocolate Chip Cookies

Pictured on page 79.

- ½ cup granulated sugar
- ½ cup packed brown sugar
- ⅓ cup margarine or butter, softened
- ⅓ cup shortening
- 1 egg
- 1 teaspoon vanilla
- 1½ cups all-purpose* or whole wheat flour
- ½ teaspoon baking soda
- ½ teaspoon salt
- ½ cup chopped nuts
- 1 package (6 ounces) semisweet chocolate chips

Heat oven to 375°. Mix sugars, margarine, shortening, egg and vanilla. Stir in remaining ingredients. Drop by rounded teaspoonfuls about 2 inches apart onto ungreased cookie sheet. Bake until light brown, 8 to 10 minutes. Cool slightly; remove from cookie sheet. ABOUT 3½ DOZEN.

*If using self-rising flour, omit baking soda and salt.

Peppermint-Chocolate Chip Cookies: Stir in ⅓ cup crushed peppermint candy.

Salted Peanut Cookies: Substitute 1 cup salted peanuts for the nuts and chocolate chips. Before baking, flatten each cookie with greased bottom of glass dipped in sugar.

Quick Cookie Stir-ins

Prepare ½ package (35.5-ounce size) chocolate chip cookie mix (1 pouch and 1 Flavor Packet) as directed except—stir in one of the following:

- ½ cup chopped walnuts
- ½ cup raisins
- ½ cup shredded or flaked coconut
- ½ cup peanut butter chips
- ½ cup butterscotch chips
- ½ cup cut-up dates
- ½ cup almond brickle chips
- 1 tablespoon grated orange peel
- ¾ teaspoon ground cinnamon and
  - ¼ teaspoon ground nutmeg

Chocolate Chip-Cereal Drops

- 1 cup packed brown sugar
- ½ cup margarine or butter, softened
- 1 egg
- 1 teaspoon vanilla
- 1 cup all-purpose flour*
- ½ teaspoon baking soda
- ½ teaspoon salt
- 1 package (6 ounces) semisweet chocolate chips
- 1 cup whole wheat flake cereal, crushed
- ½ cup chopped nuts
- ½ cup raisins

Heat oven to 350°. Mix brown sugar, margarine, egg and vanilla. Stir in remaining ingredients. Drop by rounded teaspoonfuls about 2 inches apart onto ungreased cookie sheet. Bake 12 to 15 minutes. Immediately remove from cookie sheet. ABOUT 4 DOZEN.

*If using self-rising flour, omit baking soda and salt.

Chocolate Oatmeal Drops

- 1½ cups sugar
- ½ cup margarine or butter, softened
- ½ cup shortening
- ¼ cup water
- 1 egg
- 1 teaspoon vanilla
- 3 cups quick-cooking oats
- 1 cup all-purpose flour*
- ⅓ cup cocoa
- ½ teaspoon baking soda
- ½ teaspoon salt
- 1 package (6 ounces) semisweet chocolate chips

Heat oven to 350°. Mix sugar, margarine, shortening, water, egg and vanilla. Stir in remaining ingredients. Drop by rounded teaspoonfuls about 1 inch apart onto ungreased cookie sheet. Bake until almost no indentation remains when touched, 10 to 12 minutes. Immediately remove from cookie sheet. ABOUT 6 DOZEN.

*If using self-rising flour, omit baking soda and salt.

Brown Sugar Drops

```
1   cup packed brown sugar
½   cup shortening
¼   cup buttermilk or water
1   egg
1¾  cups all-purpose* or whole wheat flour
½   teaspoon baking soda
½   teaspoon salt
    Light Brown Glaze (below)
```

Mix brown sugar, shortening, buttermilk and egg. Stir in flour, baking soda and salt. Cover and refrigerate at least 1 hour. (If using whole wheat flour, do not refrigerate.)

Heat oven to 400°. Drop by rounded teaspoonfuls about 2 inches apart onto ungreased cookie sheet. Bake until almost no indentation remains when touched, 8 to 10 minutes. Immediately remove from cookie sheet; cool. Spread cookies with Light Brown Glaze. ABOUT 3 DOZEN.

*If using self-rising flour, omit baking soda and salt.

LIGHT BROWN GLAZE

Heat ¼ cup margarine or butter over medium heat until delicate brown; remove from heat. Stir in 2 cups powdered sugar and 1 teaspoon vanilla. Beat in 1 to 2 tablespoons milk until smooth and of desired consistency.

Applesauce-Brown Sugar Drops: Substitute ½ cup applesauce for the buttermilk. Stir in 1 teaspoon ground cinnamon, ¼ teaspoon ground cloves and 1 cup raisins. ABOUT 4 DOZEN.

Chocolate Chip-Cherry Drops: Stir in ½ cup semisweet chocolate chips and ½ cup chopped maraschino cherries. Omit glaze. ABOUT 4 DOZEN.

Coconut Drops: Stir in ½ cup shredded coconut.

Holiday Fruit Drops: Stir in 1 cup candied cherries, cut into halves, 1 cup cut-up dates and ¾ cup broken pecans. Press pecan half in each cookie before baking. Omit glaze. ABOUT 4 DOZEN.

Jeweled Drops: Stir in 1½ to 2 cups cut-up gumdrops. Omit glaze.

Wheat Cereal Drops: Decrease flour to 1 cup. Stir in 1 cup oats, ½ cup whole wheat flake cereal and ½ cup coarsely chopped salted peanuts. Bake 12 to 14 minutes.

Brown Sugar Pecan Rounds

```
1¼  cups packed brown sugar
½   cup margarine or butter, softened
1   egg
1¼  cups all-purpose flour*
¼   teaspoon baking soda
⅛   teaspoon salt
½   cup coarsely chopped pecans
```

Heat oven to 350°. Mix brown sugar, margarine and egg. Stir in remaining ingredients. Drop by teaspoonfuls about 2 inches apart onto ungreased cookie sheet (dough will flatten and spread). Bake until set, 12 to 15 minutes. ABOUT 3 DOZEN.

*If using self-rising flour, omit baking soda and salt.

French Lace Crisps

```
⅔   cup packed brown sugar
½   cup light corn syrup
½   cup shortening
1   cup all-purpose flour*
1   cup finely chopped nuts
```

Heat oven to 375°. Heat brown sugar, corn syrup and shortening to boiling over medium heat, stirring constantly; remove from heat. Stir in flour and nuts gradually. Keep batter warm over hot water. Drop by teaspoonfuls about 3 inches apart onto lightly greased cookie sheet. Bake only 8 or 9 cookies at a time. Bake until set, about 5 minutes. Let stand 3 to 5 minutes; remove from cookie sheet. ABOUT 4 DOZEN.

*Do not use self-rising flour in this recipe.

Salted Peanut Crisps

1½ cups packed brown sugar
½ cup margarine or butter, softened
½ cup shortening
2 eggs
2 teaspoons vanilla
3 cups all-purpose flour *
1 teaspoon salt
½ teaspoon baking soda
2 cups salted peanuts

Heat oven to 375°. Mix brown sugar, margarine, shortening, eggs and vanilla. Stir in remaining ingredients. Drop by rounded teaspoonfuls about 2 inches apart onto lightly greased cookie sheet; flatten with greased bottom of glass dipped in sugar. Bake until golden brown, 8 to 10 minutes. Immediately remove from cookie sheet.   ABOUT 6 DOZEN.

*If using self-rising flour, omit salt and baking soda.

Chocolate Chip Peanut Crisps: Stir in 1 package (6 ounces) semisweet chocolate chips.

Spicy Peanut Drops

½ cup granulated sugar
½ cup packed brown sugar
½ cup shortening
½ cup peanut butter
½ cup milk
1 egg
1½ cups all-purpose flour *
½ teaspoon baking powder
½ teaspoon ground allspice
¼ teaspoon baking soda
¼ teaspoon salt
1 cup salted peanuts

Heat oven to 375°. Mix sugars, shortening, peanut butter, milk and egg. Stir in remaining ingredients. Drop by tablespoonfuls about 2 inches apart onto ungreased cookie sheet. Bake until golden brown, 12 to 14 minutes. ABOUT 4 DOZEN.

*If using self-rising flour, omit baking powder, baking soda and salt.

Sesame Seed Drops

½ cup margarine or butter
⅓ cup sesame seed
½ cup margarine or butter, softened
1 cup sugar
1 egg
2 tablespoons water
2 cups all-purpose flour *
1 teaspoon baking powder
¼ teaspoon salt
   Sesame Frosting (below)

Heat oven to 375°. Heat ½ cup margarine and the sesame seed over low heat, stirring occasionally, until margarine is golden brown (watch carefully to avoid burning); remove from heat. Remove 2 tablespoons sesame seed, draining margarine. Reserve remaining sesame seed mixture.

Mix the 2 tablespoons sesame seed, ½ cup softened margarine, the sugar, egg and water. Stir in flour, baking powder and salt. Drop by rounded teaspoonfuls about 2 inches apart onto ungreased cookie sheet; flatten each with greased bottom of glass dipped in sugar. Bake until edges are light brown, about 10 minutes; cool. Frost with Sesame Frosting.   ABOUT 3 DOZEN.

*If using self-rising flour, omit baking powder and salt.

SESAME FROSTING
Beat 3 cups powdered sugar, 3 tablespoons milk, 1 teaspoon vanilla and the reserved sesame seed mixture until frosting is of spreading consistency.

Almond-Cherry Macaroons

1¼ cups diced roasted almonds
¾ cup sugar
3 egg whites
¼ cup chopped maraschino cherries,
    well drained

Mix almonds, sugar and egg whites in saucepan. Cook over medium heat, stirring constantly, until path remains when spoon is drawn through mixture, 6 to 8 minutes; remove from heat. Stir in cherries.

Heat oven to 300°. Drop mixture by rounded teaspoonfuls about 1 inch apart onto lightly greased and floured cookie sheet. Let stand at room temperature until cool (to ensure rounded cookies). Bake until light brown, about 20 minutes. Immediately remove from cookie sheet. ABOUT 1½ DOZEN.

Almond Macaroons: Omit cherries. Stir in 2 to 3 teaspoons almond extract.

Coconut-Apricot Drops

1 cup coarsely cut-up dried apricots
½ cup water
½ cup granulated sugar
½ cup packed brown sugar
½ cup margarine or butter, softened
½ cup shortening
1 egg
1 teaspoon vanilla
½ teaspoon almond extract
1¾ cups all-purpose flour*
2 teaspoons baking powder
½ teaspoon salt
    About 1½ cups flaked coconut

Cook apricots and water over low heat until water is absorbed, about 15 minutes; cool. Heat oven to 350°. Mix sugars, margarine, shortening, egg, vanilla and almond extract. Stir in apricots, flour, baking powder and salt. Drop by rounded teaspoonfuls into coconut; roll around to coat. Place about 2 inches apart on ungreased cookie sheet. Press toasted whole almond in each cookie if desired. Bake until light brown, 12 to 13 minutes. ABOUT 5 DOZEN.

*If using self-rising flour, omit baking powder and salt.

Coconut-Carrot Cookies

The next time you cook carrots for dinner, cook more than you need and bake these cookies.

1 cup mashed cooked carrots (about 4 medium)
¾ cup sugar
½ cup margarine or butter, softened
½ cup shortening
2 eggs
2 cups all-purpose* or whole wheat flour
2 teaspoons baking powder
½ teaspoon salt
¾ cup shredded or flaked coconut
    Orange Butter Frosting (below)

Heat oven to 400°. Mix carrots, sugar, margarine, shortening and eggs. Stir in flour, baking powder and salt. Mix in coconut. Drop by rounded teaspoonfuls about 2 inches apart onto ungreased cookie sheet. Bake until almost no indentation remains when touched, 8 to 10 minutes. Immediately remove from cookie sheet; cool. Frost with Orange Butter Frosting. ABOUT 5 DOZEN.

*If using self-rising flour, omit baking powder and salt.

ORANGE BUTTER FROSTING
Mix 1½ cups powdered sugar and 3 tablespoons margarine or butter, softened. Beat in 2 teaspoons grated orange peel and about 1 tablespoon orange juice until frosting is of spreading consistency.

Coconut Meringues

4 egg whites (½ cup)
1¼ cups sugar
½ teaspoon vanilla
¼ teaspoon salt
2½ cups shredded or flaked coconut

Heat oven to 325°. Beat egg whites in large mixer bowl on high speed until foamy. Beat in sugar gradually; continue beating until stiff and glossy. Do not underbeat. Stir in remaining ingredients. Drop by generous teaspoonfuls about 2 inches apart onto waxed paper-lined or lightly greased cookie sheet. Bake until set and delicate brown, about 20 minutes. Immediately remove from waxed paper. ABOUT 3 DOZEN.

Coconut-Cherry Drops

      1 cup sugar
      ½ cup margarine or butter, softened
      ½ cup shortening
      ½ cup dairy sour cream
      3 eggs
    3¼ cups all-purpose flour
    1½ teaspoons salt
      1 teaspoon baking powder
      ½ teaspoon baking soda
    1½ teaspoons lemon or almond extract
      1 teaspoon grated orange peel
      1 cup shredded coconut
      ½ cup cut-up candied cherries
      ¼ cup cut-up citron

Heat oven to 400°. Mix sugar, margarine, shortening, sour cream and eggs. Stir in remaining ingredients. Drop by rounded teaspoonfuls about 2 inches apart onto ungreased cookie sheet. Bake until light brown, 8 to 9 minutes. ABOUT 6 DOZEN.

Coconut-Rhubarb Drops

      ½ cup shortening
      ¼ cup sugar
      ¾ cup light corn syrup
      1 egg
      1 cup cooked rhubarb
      2 cups all-purpose flour
      1 teaspoon baking powder
      1 teaspoon ground nutmeg
      ½ teaspoon baking soda
      ½ teaspoon salt
      ¼ teaspoon ground cloves
      1 cup coconut
      ½ cup raisins
      ½ cup chopped nuts

Heat oven to 375°. Mix shortening, sugar, corn syrup, egg and rhubarb. Stir in flour, baking powder, nutmeg, baking soda, salt and cloves. Mix in remaining ingredients. Drop by generous teaspoonfuls about 2 inches apart onto greased cookie sheet. Bake 15 to 18 minutes. ABOUT 5½ DOZEN.

Peach-Coconut Drops: Substitute 1 can (16 ounces) sliced peaches, drained and chopped, for the rhubarb.

Soft Molasses Drops

      1 cup sugar
      1 cup shortening
      ½ cup molasses
      1 egg
      3 cups all-purpose flour*
      ¾ cup dairy sour cream
      2 teaspoons baking soda
      1 teaspoon salt
      1 teaspoon ground ginger
      1 teaspoon ground cinnamon

Heat oven to 375°. Mix sugar, shortening, molasses and egg. Stir in remaining ingredients. Drop by rounded teaspoonfuls about 2 inches apart onto ungreased cookie sheet. Bake about 8 minutes. ABOUT 5 DOZEN.

*If using self-rising flour, omit baking soda and salt.

Ginger Creams

      ½ cup sugar
      ½ cup molasses
      ½ cup water
      ⅓ cup shortening
      1 egg
      2 cups all-purpose* or whole wheat flour
      1 teaspoon ground ginger
      ½ teaspoon salt
      ½ teaspoon baking soda
      ½ teaspoon ground nutmeg
      ½ teaspoon ground cloves
      ½ teaspoon ground cinnamon
        Vanilla Frosting (page 54)

Mix sugar, molasses, water, shortening and egg. Stir in remaining ingredients except frosting. Cover and refrigerate at least 1 hour.

Heat oven to 400°. Drop by teaspoonfuls about 2 inches apart onto ungreased cookie sheet. Bake until almost no indentation remains when touched, about 8 minutes. Immediately remove from cookie sheet; cool. Frost with Vanilla Frosting. ABOUT 4 DOZEN.

*If using self-rising flour, omit salt and baking soda.

Quick Ginger Drops

Heat oven to 375°. Mix 1 package (14.5 ounces) gingerbread mix and ½ cup water. Drop by teaspoonfuls onto lightly greased cookie sheet. Bake 10 to 12 minutes. ABOUT 3 DOZEN.

Chocolate Chip Ginger Drops: Stir in 1 package (6 ounces) semisweet chocolate chips and ½ cup chopped nuts.

Coconut-Ginger Drops: Stir in 1 cup shredded coconut.

Date-Nut Ginger Drops: Stir in ½ cup cut-up dates and ½ cup chopped nuts.

Fruit Ginger Drops: Stir in 1 cup cut-up candied fruit and ½ cup chopped nuts.

Granola Ginger Drops: Stir in 1 cup granola and ½ cup chopped nuts. ABOUT 3½ DOZEN.

Jeweled Ginger Drops: Stir in ⅔ cup cut-up gumdrops and ½ cup chopped nuts.

Mincemeat Ginger Drops: Stir in 1 cup prepared mincemeat and ½ cup chopped nuts. ABOUT 4 DOZEN.

Orange-Coconut Ginger Drops: Omit water. Stir in 1 cup shredded coconut, 1 tablespoon grated orange peel and juice from 1 orange plus enough water to measure ½ cup.

Peanut Butter Ginger Drops: Stir in ½ cup peanut butter.

Peanut Ginger Drops: Stir in 1 cup chopped peanuts.

Raisin-Nut Ginger Drops: Stir in 1 cup raisins and ½ cup chopped nuts.

Monkey-faced Cookies

    1   cup packed brown sugar
    ½   cup shortening
    ½   cup molasses
    ½   cup milk
    1   teaspoon vinegar
    2½ cups all-purpose flour *
    1   teaspoon baking soda
    ½   teaspoon salt
    ½   teaspoon ground ginger
    ½   teaspoon ground cinnamon
        Raisins

Heat oven to 375°. Mix brown sugar, shortening, molasses, milk and vinegar. Stir in flour, baking soda, salt, ginger and cinnamon. Drop by rounded teaspoonfuls about 2 inches apart onto ungreased cookie sheet. Press 3 raisins in each cookie for eyes and mouth. Bake until set, 11 to 12 minutes. ABOUT 5 DOZEN.

*If using self-rising flour, decrease baking soda to ¼ teaspoon and omit salt.

Raisin-Cherry Drops

    1½ cups raisins
    1   cup water
    1½ cups sugar
    ¾   cup shortening
    2   eggs
    3   cups all-purpose flour *
    1½ teaspoons salt
    1   teaspoon ground cinnamon
    ¾   teaspoon baking powder
    ¾   teaspoon baking soda
    ¼   teaspoon ground allspice
    ¼   teaspoon ground nutmeg
    ¾   cup chopped nuts
    ½   cup chopped maraschino cherries

Heat oven to 400°. Heat raisins and water to boiling, stirring occasionally. Boil 5 minutes. Drain, reserving ⅓ cup liquid. Mix sugar, shortening, eggs and reserved liquid. Stir in raisins and the remaining ingredients. Drop by rounded teaspoonfuls about 2 inches apart onto ungreased cookie sheet. Bake until light brown, 8 to 10 minutes. Immediately remove from cookie sheet. ABOUT 7½ DOZEN.

*If using self-rising flour, omit salt, baking powder and baking soda.

Applesauce-Raisin Drops

    1   cup packed brown sugar
    ¾   cup shortening
    ½   cup applesauce
    1   egg
    2¼ cups all-purpose flour*
    ¾   teaspoon ground cinnamon
    ½   teaspoon baking soda
    ½   teaspoon salt
    ¼   teaspoon ground cloves
    1   cup raisins
    ½   cup chopped nuts

Heat oven to 375°. Mix brown sugar, shortening, applesauce and egg. Stir in remaining ingredients. Drop by rounded teaspoonfuls about 2 inches apart onto ungreased cookie sheet. Bake until almost no indentation remains when touched, 11 to 12 minutes. ABOUT 5 DOZEN.

*If using self-rising flour, omit baking soda and salt.

Applesauce-Spice Drops

    2   cups packed brown sugar
    1   cup shortening
    ½   cup cold coffee
    1   can (16½ ounces) applesauce
    2   eggs
    3½ cups all-purpose flour*
    1   teaspoon baking soda
    1   teaspoon salt
    1   teaspoon ground cinnamon
    1   teaspoon ground nutmeg
    1   teaspoon ground cloves
    1   cup raisins
    ½   cup coarsely chopped nuts

Heat oven to 400°. Mix brown sugar, shortening, coffee, applesauce and eggs. Stir in remaining ingredients (dough will be very soft). Drop by rounded teaspoonfuls about 2 inches apart onto lightly greased cookie sheet. Bake until almost no indentation remains when touched, about 7 minutes. ABOUT 7 DOZEN.

*If using self-rising flour, omit baking soda and salt.

Coffee-Apple Drops

    2   cups finely chopped pared apples
    1   cup sugar
    1   cup strong coffee*
    1   cup raisins
    ½   cup shortening
    1   teaspoon ground cinnamon
    ¾   teaspoon ground cloves
    ¾   teaspoon ground nutmeg
    2   cups all-purpose flour**
    1   teaspoon baking soda
    1   teaspoon vanilla
    ¼   teaspoon salt
    1   cup chopped nuts

Heat oven to 375°. Cook apples, sugar, coffee, raisins, shortening, cinnamon, cloves and nutmeg over medium heat until apples are tender, about 10 minutes; remove from heat. Cool; stir in remaining ingredients. Drop by rounded teaspoonfuls about 2 inches apart onto ungreased cookie sheet. Bake until light brown, about 10 minutes. ABOUT 5½ DOZEN.

* 1 tablespoon powdered instant coffee dissolved in 1 cup water can be substituted for the 1 cup strong coffee.
** If using self-rising flour, omit baking soda and salt.

Cinnamon-Raisin Drops

    1½ cups packed brown sugar
    ½   cup shortening
    ½   cup margarine or butter, softened
    3   eggs
    3   cups all-purpose flour*
    2   teaspoons ground cinnamon
    1   teaspoon baking soda
    1   teaspoon salt
    1   teaspoon ground cloves
    1   cup raisins
    1   cup chopped nuts

Heat oven to 375°. Mix brown sugar, shortening, margarine and eggs. Stir in remaining ingredients. Drop by teaspoonfuls about 2 inches apart onto greased cookie sheet. Bake about 10 minutes. ABOUT 5 DOZEN.

*If using self-rising flour, omit baking soda and salt.

Banana-Spice Drops

    1 cup packed brown sugar
    1 cup mashed bananas (2 to 3 medium)
   ¼ cup margarine or butter, softened
   ¼ cup shortening
    2 eggs
    2 cups all-purpose flour*
    2 teaspoons baking powder
   ½ teaspoon ground cinnamon
   ¼ teaspoon ground cloves
   ¼ teaspoon baking soda
   ¼ teaspoon salt
   ½ cup chopped nuts
      Cherry Frosting (below), Chocolate
         Frosting (page 45) or Vanilla Frosting
         (page 54)

Mix brown sugar, bananas, margarine, shortening and eggs. Stir in remaining ingredients except frosting. Cover and refrigerate at least 1 hour.

Heat oven to 375°. Drop by rounded teaspoonfuls about 2 inches apart onto lightly greased cookie sheet. Bake until almost no indentation remains when touched, 8 to 10 minutes. Immediately remove from cookie sheet; cool. Frost cookies with Cherry Frosting. 4 DOZEN.

*If using self-rising flour, omit baking powder, baking soda and salt.

CHERRY FROSTING
    3 cups powdered sugar
   ⅓ cup margarine or butter, softened
    2 tablespoons drained chopped
         maraschino cherries
   1½ teaspoons vanilla
    2 drops red food color
      About 2 tablespoons milk

Mix powdered sugar and margarine. Beat in cherries, vanilla, food color and milk until of spreading consistency.

Banana-Oatmeal Drops

   1¾ cups oats
   1½ cups all-purpose flour*
    1 cup sugar
    1 cup mashed bananas (2 to 3 medium)
   ¾ cup shortening
    1 egg
    1 teaspoon salt
    1 teaspoon ground cinnamon
   ½ teaspoon baking soda
   ¼ teaspoon ground nutmeg
   ½ cup chopped nuts or raisins

Heat oven to 400°. Mix all ingredients. Drop by rounded teaspoonfuls about 2 inches apart onto ungreased cookie sheet. Bake until light brown, about 10 minutes.   ABOUT 4 DOZEN.

*If using self-rising flour, omit salt and baking soda.

Banana-Chocolate Chip Drops: Substitute semisweet chocolate chips for the nuts.

Banana-Granola Drops: Heat oven to 375°. Omit oats and nuts. Mix in 2 cups granola and 1 teaspoon vanilla. Bake until almost no indentation remains when touched, 8 to 10 minutes. Immediately remove from cookie sheet.   ABOUT 3½ DOZEN.

Spiced Prune Drops

    1 cup packed brown sugar
   ½ cup margarine or butter, softened
   ¼ cup milk
    1 egg
   1¾ cups all-purpose flour*
   ½ teaspoon baking soda
   ½ teaspoon salt
   ½ teaspoon ground nutmeg
   ½ teaspoon ground cinnamon
   ⅛ teaspoon ground cloves
    1 cup cut-up dried prunes
   ½ cup chopped nuts

Heat oven to 400°. Mix brown sugar, margarine, milk and egg. Stir in remaining ingredients. Drop by rounded teaspoonfuls about 2 inches apart onto ungreased cookie sheet. Bake until almost no indentation remains when touched, 8 to 9 minutes.   ABOUT 4½ DOZEN.

*If using self-rising flour, omit baking soda and salt.

Soft Pumpkin Drops

1 cup sugar
1 cup canned pumpkin
½ cup shortening
1 tablespoon grated orange peel
2 cups all-purpose* or whole wheat flour
1 teaspoon baking powder
1 teaspoon baking soda
1 teaspoon ground cinnamon
¼ teaspoon salt
½ cup raisins
½ cup chopped nuts
Vanilla Frosting (below)

Heat oven to 375°. Mix sugar, pumpkin, shortening and orange peel. Stir in flour, baking powder, baking soda, cinnamon and salt. Mix in raisins and nuts. Drop by rounded teaspoonfuls about 2 inches apart onto ungreased cookie sheet. Bake until light brown, 8 to 10 minutes; cool. Frost with Vanilla Frosting. ABOUT 4 DOZEN.

*If using self-rising flour, omit baking powder, baking soda and salt.

VANILLA FROSTING

Mix 3 cups powdered sugar and ⅓ cup margarine or butter, softened. Beat in 1½ teaspoons vanilla and about 2 tablespoons milk until smooth and of spreading consistency.

Chocolate Chip Pumpkin Drops: Substitute semisweet chocolate chips for the raisins or nuts.

Made with Whole Wheat Flour

Pumpkin-Pecan Drops

1½ cups packed brown sugar
½ cup shortening
2 eggs
1 can (16 ounces) pumpkin
2¾ cups all-purpose flour*
3 teaspoons baking powder
1 teaspoon ground cinnamon
½ teaspoon salt
½ teaspoon ground nutmeg
¼ teaspoon ground ginger
1 cup raisins
1 cup chopped pecans

Heat oven to 400°. Mix brown sugar, shortening, eggs and pumpkin. Stir in remaining ingredients. Drop by teaspoonfuls about 2 inches apart onto ungreased cookie sheet. Bake until light brown, 12 to 15 minutes. Immediately remove from cookie sheet. ABOUT 6 DOZEN.

*If using self-rising flour, omit baking powder and salt.

Cranberry Drops

1 cup granulated sugar
¾ cup packed brown sugar
½ cup margarine or butter, softened
¼ cup milk
2 tablespoons orange juice
1 egg
3 cups all-purpose flour*
1 teaspoon baking powder
½ teaspoon salt
¼ teaspoon baking soda
2½ cups coarsely chopped frozen cranberries
1 cup chopped nuts

Heat oven to 375°. Mix sugars and margarine. Stir in milk, orange juice and egg. Mix in remaining ingredients. Drop by rounded teaspoonfuls about 2 inches apart onto greased cookie sheet. Bake 10 to 15 minutes. ABOUT 5½ DOZEN.

*If using self-rising flour, omit salt and baking soda.

Glazed Date Drops

¾ cup packed brown sugar
½ cup dairy sour cream
¼ cup margarine or butter, softened
1 egg
½ teaspoon vanilla
1¼ cups all-purpose flour*
½ teaspoon baking soda
¼ teaspoon baking powder
1 package (8 ounces) dates, cut up
½ cup chopped walnuts
   Satin Glaze (below)

Heat oven to 400°. Mix brown sugar, sour cream, margarine, egg and vanilla. Stir in flour, baking soda and baking powder. Mix in dates and walnuts. Drop by teaspoonfuls about 2 inches apart onto lightly greased cookie sheet. Bake about 10 minutes; cool. Spread with Satin Glaze. ABOUT 4 DOZEN.

*If using self-rising flour, omit baking soda and baking powder.

SATIN GLAZE

Heat ½ cup margarine or butter in saucepan until melted; remove from heat. Stir in 3 cups powdered sugar and 1 teaspoon vanilla. Beat in 3 to 4 tablespoons hot water, 1 tablespoon at a time, until smooth and of desired consistency.

Quick Date Drops

1 package (14 ounces) date bar mix
¼ cup hot water
1 egg

Heat oven to 400°. Mix date mix and hot water. Mix in crumb mix and egg. Drop by rounded teaspoonfuls about 2 inches apart onto lightly greased cookie sheet. Bake 8 to 10 minutes. ABOUT 2½ DOZEN.

Cinnamon-Nut Drops: Stir in ½ cup chopped nuts and ½ teaspoon ground cinnamon.

Cinnamon-Raisin Drops: Stir in 1 cup raisins and ½ teaspoon ground cinnamon. ABOUT 3½ DOZEN.

Nut-Raisin Drops: Stir in 1 cup raisins, ½ cup chopped nuts and ½ teaspoon ground cinnamon. ABOUT 3½ DOZEN.

Pineapple-Date Drops: Substitute 1 can (8¼ ounces) crushed pineapple (with syrup) for the hot water. Stir in ½ cup chopped nuts. ABOUT 3½ DOZEN.

Quick Fruit Drops: Heat oven to 375°. Stir in 1 cup broken pecans or walnuts, 1 cup candied cherries, cut into halves, and ½ teaspoon ground cinnamon. ABOUT 3 DOZEN.

Quick Orange-Raisin Drops: Heat oven to 375°. Stir in 1 tablespoon grated orange peel, 1 tablespoon grated lemon peel, 1 cup chopped walnuts and 1 cup raisins. Bake 10 to 12 minutes. ABOUT 4 DOZEN.

Orange Drops

¾ cup sugar
⅔ cup shortening
2 tablespoons grated orange peel
½ cup orange juice
1 egg
2 cups all-purpose flour*
½ teaspoon baking powder
½ teaspoon baking soda
½ teaspoon salt

Heat oven to 400°. Mix sugar, shortening, orange peel, orange juice and egg. Stir in remaining ingredients. Drop by rounded teaspoonfuls about 2 inches apart onto ungreased cookie sheet. Bake until edges are light brown, 8 to 9 minutes; cool. Frost with Orange Frosting (below) if desired. ABOUT 3½ DOZEN.

*If using self-rising flour, omit baking powder, baking soda and salt.

ORANGE FROSTING

Mix 2 cups powdered sugar and 2 tablespoons margarine or butter, softened. Beat in 1 tablespoon grated orange peel and about 2 tablespoons orange juice until well mixed and of spreading consistency.

Orange-Nut Drops: Stir in ½ cup chopped nuts.

Orange-Raisin Drops: Stir in ½ cup raisins.

Pineapple Puffs

1½ cups sugar
 ½ cup shortening
 ½ cup dairy sour cream
  1 egg
  1 can (8¼ ounces) crushed pineapple
3½ cups all-purpose flour*
  1 teaspoon baking soda
  1 teaspoon vanilla
 ½ teaspoon salt
 ½ cup chopped nuts
     Glaze (below)

Heat oven to 400°. Mix sugar, shortening, sour cream, egg and pineapple (with syrup). Stir in flour, baking soda, vanilla, salt and nuts. Drop by teaspoonfuls about 2 inches apart onto ungreased cookie sheet. Bake until almost no indentation remains when touched, 8 to 10 minutes. Immediately remove from cookie sheet; cool. Spread with Glaze.   ABOUT 6 DOZEN.

*If using self-rising flour, omit baking soda and salt.

GLAZE
Beat 2 cups powdered sugar, 1 teaspoon vanilla and about 4 tablespoons milk until smooth and of desired consistency.

Pineapple Drops

1½ cups sugar
  1 cup shortening
  1 egg
  1 can (8¼ ounces) crushed pineapple
3½ cups all-purpose flour*
  1 teaspoon baking soda
 ½ teaspoon salt
 ¼ teaspoon ground nutmeg
 ½ cup chopped macadamia nuts, walnuts
     or pecans

Heat oven to 400°. Mix sugar, shortening and egg. Stir in pineapple (with syrup) and the remaining ingredients. Drop by rounded teaspoonfuls about 2 inches apart onto ungreased cookie sheet. Bake until golden brown and no indentation remains when touched, 8 to 10 minutes.   ABOUT 5 DOZEN.

*If using self-rising flour, omit baking soda and salt.

Pineapple-Coconut Drops: Omit nutmeg. Stir in 1 cup flaked coconut.

Pineapple-Raisin Drops: Stir in 1 cup raisins.

Fruit-filled Drops

Pictured at right.

     Date Filling or Pineapple-Cherry Filling
       (below)
  2 cups packed brown sugar
  1 cup shortening
  2 eggs
 ½ cup water or buttermilk
  1 teaspoon vanilla
3½ cups all-purpose flour*
  1 teaspoon salt
  1 teaspoon baking soda
 ⅛ teaspoon ground cinnamon

Prepare Date Filling; cool. Heat oven to 400°. Mix brown sugar, shortening and eggs. Stir in water and vanilla. Mix in remaining ingredients. Drop by teaspoonfuls about 2 inches apart onto ungreased cookie sheet. Top each teaspoonful of dough with ½ teaspoon filling. Top filling with ½ teaspoon dough. Bake 10 to 12 minutes. Immediately remove from cookie sheet.   ABOUT 5½ DOZEN.

*If using self-rising flour, omit salt and baking soda.

DATE FILLING
Cook 2 cups snipped dates, ¾ cup sugar and ¾ cup water over low heat, stirring constantly, until thickened. Stir in ½ cup chopped nuts.

PINEAPPLE-CHERRY FILLING
Cook 1 can (8¼ ounces) crushed pineapple (with syrup), ¼ cup cut-up candied cherries or chopped maraschino cherries and ½ cup sugar in saucepan over low heat, stirring constantly, until thickened. Stir in ½ cup chopped nuts.

Drop dough by teaspoonfuls about 2 inches apart onto cookie sheet.

Top each teaspoonful of dough with ½ teaspoon filling.

Cover with ½ teaspoon dough; dough will spread as cookie bakes.

Fruit-filled Drops (page 56)

Sour Cream Drops, Candy Drops and Fruit Drops (all on page 59)

Sour Cream Drops

Sour Cream Drops, Candy Drops and Fruit Drops—*pictured at left.*

2¾ cups all-purpose flour*
1½ cups packed brown sugar
 1 cup dairy sour cream
 ½ cup shortening
 1 teaspoon salt
 1 teaspoon vanilla
 ½ teaspoon baking soda
 2 eggs
 1 cup chopped nuts, if desired
    Maple Butter Glaze (below)

Mix all ingredients except glaze. (If dough is soft, cover and refrigerate.) Heat oven to 375°. Drop by level tablespoonfuls about 2 inches apart onto ungreased cookie sheet. Bake until almost no indentation remains when touched, about 10 minutes. Immediately remove from cookie sheet; cool. Spread with Maple Butter Glaze. 4½ TO 5 DOZEN.

*If using self-rising flour, omit salt and baking soda.

MAPLE BUTTER GLAZE
Heat ½ cup butter over low heat until golden brown; remove from heat. Stir in 2 cups powdered sugar and 2 teaspoons maple flavoring. Beat in 2 to 4 tablespoons hot water until smooth and of desired consistency.

Applesauce Drops: Omit sour cream. Mix in ¾ cup applesauce, 1 teaspoon ground cinnamon, ¼ teaspoon ground cloves and 1 cup raisins.

Candy Drops: Omit nuts. Mix in 4 cups cut-up gumdrops. Drop dough by tablespoonfuls onto greased and floured cookie sheet. Omit glaze. ABOUT 6 DOZEN.

Chocolate-Cherry Drops: Mix in ½ cup semisweet chocolate chips and ½ cup chopped maraschino cherries.

Chocolate Chip Drops: Stir in 1 package (6 ounces) semisweet chocolate chips.

Coconut Sour Cream Drops: Substitute shredded coconut for the nuts.

Date-filled Drops: Cook 1 cup cut-up dates, ⅓ cup sugar and ⅓ cup water over low heat, stirring constantly, until thickened. Stir in ¼ cup chopped nuts; cool. Top level tablespoonfuls of dough with ½ teaspoon filling. Top filling with 1 teaspoon dough. Omit glaze. ABOUT 4 DOZEN.

Fruit Drops: Omit nuts. Mix in 2 cups candied cherries, cut into halves, 2 cups cut-up dates and 1½ cups chopped walnuts. Drop by rounded teaspoonfuls onto ungreased cookie sheet. Press walnut half in each cookie. Omit glaze. ABOUT 7 DOZEN.

Maple Drops: Substitute 1 tablespoon maple flavoring for the vanilla.

Peanut Drops: Substitute salted peanuts for the nuts.

Raisin Sour Cream Drops: Mix in 1 cup raisins.

Spicy Sugar Drops: Mix ½ cup sugar, 1 teaspoon ground cinnamon and ¼ teaspoon ground cloves; sprinkle over cookies before baking. Omit glaze.

Spicy Fruit Drops

 ½ cup molasses
 ⅓ cup shortening
 ¼ cup sugar
 1 egg
1½ cups all-purpose flour*
 1 teaspoon ground cinnamon
 1 teaspoon ground mace
 1 teaspoon ground nutmeg
 ½ teaspoon baking soda
 ¼ teaspoon salt
 ¼ teaspoon ground ginger
 ¼ teaspoon ground allspice
2½ cups mixed candied fruit (about 16
    ounces)
 2 cups coarsely chopped nuts

Heat oven to 325°. Mix molasses, shortening, sugar and egg. Stir in remaining ingredients. Drop by teaspoonfuls about 1 inch apart onto lightly greased cookie sheet. Bake 12 to 15 minutes. ABOUT 6 DOZEN.

*If using self-rising flour, omit baking soda and salt.

Spiced Bran Drops

    1   cup packed brown sugar
    ¼   cup margarine or butter, softened
    ¼   cup shortening
    ¼   cup cold coffee
    1   egg
    1¾ cups all-purpose flour*
    ½   teaspoon baking soda
    ½   teaspoon salt
    ½   teaspoon ground cinnamon
    ½   teaspoon ground nutmeg
    1¼ cups raisins
    1¼ cups whole bran cereal

Heat oven to 375°. Mix brown sugar, margarine, shortening, coffee and egg. Stir in remaining ingredients. Drop by rounded teaspoonfuls about 2 inches apart onto ungreased cookie sheet. Bake until almost no indentation remains when touched, 8 to 10 minutes. Immediately remove from cookie sheet. ABOUT 4 DOZEN.

*If using self-rising flour, omit baking soda and salt.

Mincemeat-Bran Drops: Stir in 1 cup prepared mincemeat.

Granola-Molasses Crisps

    2   cups granola, crushed
    ¾   cup packed brown sugar
    ½   cup margarine or butter, softened
    3   tablespoons all-purpose flour
    2   tablespoons molasses
    1   teaspoon vanilla
    ¼   teaspoon salt

Heat oven to 350°. Mix all ingredients. Drop by level teaspoonfuls about 3 inches apart onto ungreased cookie sheet. Bake only 6 cookies at a time. Bake until cookies are thin and edges are light brown, 5 to 7 minutes. Cool 3 to 4 minutes; carefully remove from cookie sheet with wide spatula. ABOUT 3½ DOZEN.

Granola-Molasses Roll-ups: Immediately roll each cookie into cylindrical shape after removing from cookie sheet. If cookies become too firm before rolling, return to oven until slightly soft, about 30 seconds.

Spiced Granola Drops

    1   cup packed brown sugar
    ½   cup granulated sugar
    ¾   cup shortening
    ¼   cup water
    1   egg
    1   teaspoon vanilla
    3   cups granola, slightly crushed
    1¼ cups all-purpose flour
    1   teaspoon salt
    1   teaspoon ground cinnamon
    ½   teaspoon baking soda
    ½   teaspoon ground cloves
    1   cup raisins
    1   cup chopped nuts, if desired

Heat oven to 350°. Mix sugars, shortening, water, egg and vanilla. Stir in remaining ingredients. Drop by rounded teaspoonfuls about 2 inches apart onto ungreased cookie sheet. Bake until almost no indentation remains when touched, 11 to 13 minutes. Cool 1 minute; remove from cookie sheet. Store in airtight container. ABOUT 5 DOZEN.

Chewy Granola Drops

    1¼ cups sugar
    ½   cup vegetable oil
    ⅓   cup molasses
    ¼   cup water
    2   eggs
    2   cups all-purpose flour*
    1   tablespoon nonfat dry milk
    1   teaspoon baking soda
    1   teaspoon salt
    1   teaspoon ground cinnamon
    2   cups granola
    1   cup raisins
    ½   cup chopped nuts

Heat oven to 375°. Mix sugar, oil, molasses, water and eggs. Stir in remaining ingredients. Drop by rounded teaspoonfuls about 2 inches apart onto lightly greased cookie sheet. Bake until almost no indentation remains when touched, 8 to 10 minutes. Cool slightly; remove from cookie sheet. ABOUT 7 DOZEN.

*If using self-rising flour, omit baking soda and salt.

Granola-Fruit Drops

½ cup packed brown sugar
¼ cup margarine or butter, softened
¼ cup shortening
¼ cup milk
2 eggs
1½ cups all-purpose flour
1 teaspoon baking powder
½ teaspoon salt
1 package (8 ounces) dates, cut up
3 cups granola
¾ cup halved candied cherries
½ cup chopped nuts, if desired

Heat oven to 375°. Mix brown sugar, margarine, shortening, milk and eggs; reserve. Mix flour, baking powder, salt and dates. Stir in granola, cherries and nuts. Stir granola mixture into brown sugar mixture. Drop by rounded teaspoonfuls about 2 inches apart onto greased cookie sheet. Press additional candied cherry half in each cookie if desired. Bake until light brown, 8 to 10 minutes. Immediately remove from cookie sheet. ABOUT 4 DOZEN.

Oatmeal-Peanut Butter Drops

½ cup granulated sugar
½ cup packed brown sugar
½ cup shortening
½ cup peanut butter
1 egg
½ teaspoon vanilla
1 cup all-purpose flour*
½ teaspoon baking soda
¼ teaspoon baking powder
¼ teaspoon salt
1½ cups quick-cooking oats

Heat oven to 375°. Mix sugars, shortening, peanut butter, egg and vanilla. Stir in remaining ingredients. Drop by rounded teaspoonfuls about 2 inches apart onto ungreased cookie sheet. Bake until golden brown, 8 to 10 minutes. Immediately remove from cookie sheet. ABOUT 3½ DOZEN.

*If using self-rising flour, omit baking soda, baking powder and salt.

Oatmeal-Orange Crunchies

2 cups all-purpose flour*
2 cups sugar
4 teaspoons baking powder
1 teaspoon salt
1 teaspoon ground nutmeg
1 cup shortening
2 eggs
1 tablespoon plus 1 teaspoon grated orange peel
2 tablespoons orange juice
3 cups oats

Heat oven to 375°. Mix flour, sugar, baking powder, salt and nutmeg. Stir in shortening, eggs, orange peel and orange juice. Mix in oats. Drop by level tablespoonfuls about 2 inches apart onto greased cookie sheet. Bake 12 to 15 minutes. ABOUT 5 DOZEN.

*If using self-rising flour, omit baking powder and salt.

Oatmeal-Wheat Flake Drops

½ cup granulated sugar
½ cup packed brown sugar
½ cup shortening
1 egg
½ teaspoon vanilla
1 cup all-purpose flour*
½ teaspoon baking soda
¼ teaspoon baking powder
¼ teaspoon salt
1 cup quick-cooking oats
1 cup whole wheat flake cereal
½ cup shredded coconut, salted peanuts or chocolate chips

Heat oven to 375°. Mix sugars, shortening, egg and vanilla. Stir in remaining ingredients thoroughly (dough will be stiff). Drop by rounded teaspoonfuls about 2 inches apart onto ungreased cookie sheet. Bake until set but not hard, 9 to 11 minutes. Cool 3 minutes; remove from cookie sheet. ABOUT 3 DOZEN.

*If using self-rising flour, omit baking soda, baking powder and salt.

Whole Wheat-Oatmeal Drops: Mix in 2 tablespoons milk with the vanilla. Substitute whole wheat flour for the all-purpose flour.

Raisin-Oatmeal Drops

- 1 cup packed brown sugar
- ½ cup granulated sugar
- ¾ cup shortening
- 1 egg
- ¼ cup water
- 1 teaspoon vanilla
- 1 cup all-purpose* or whole wheat flour
- 1 teaspoon salt
- 1 teaspoon ground cinnamon
- ½ teaspoon baking soda
- ½ teaspoon ground cloves
- 3 cups quick-cooking oats
- 1 cup raisins
- 1 cup chopped nuts

Heat oven to 350°. Mix sugars, shortening, egg, water and vanilla. Stir in remaining ingredients. Drop by rounded teaspoonfuls about 1 inch apart onto greased cookie sheet. Bake until almost no indentation remains when touched, 12 to 15 minutes. Immediately remove from cookie sheet. Store in airtight container. ABOUT 5 DOZEN.

*If using self-rising flour, omit salt and baking soda.

Banana-Oatmeal Drops: Omit water. Increase baking soda to 1 teaspoon. Stir 1 cup mashed bananas (2 to 3 medium) into shortening mixture.

Raisin Drops: Omit oats. Increase flour to 2½ cups.

Oatmeal Crispies

- ½ cup granulated sugar
- ½ cup packed brown sugar
- ¼ cup margarine or butter, softened
- ¼ cup shortening
- 1 egg
- ½ teaspoon vanilla
- 1 cup all-purpose flour*
- ½ teaspoon baking soda
- ¼ teaspoon baking powder
- ¼ teaspoon salt
- 1½ cups quick-cooking oats

Heat oven to 375°. Mix sugars, margarine, shortening, egg and vanilla. Stir in remaining ingredients. Drop by rounded teaspoonfuls about 2 inches apart onto ungreased cookie sheet. Bake 10 minutes. Immediately remove from cookie sheet. ABOUT 3 DOZEN.

*If using self-rising flour, omit baking soda, baking powder and salt.

Rich Cereal Drops

- 1 can (14 ounces) sweetened condensed milk
- ½ cup creamy peanut butter
- 2 cups crushed whole wheat flake cereal or graham cracker crumbs
- 1 package (6 ounces) semisweet chocolate chips

Heat oven to 350°. Mix milk and peanut butter until smooth. Stir in cereal and chocolate chips. Drop by rounded teaspoonfuls about 2 inches apart onto ungreased cookie sheet. Bake until light brown, 10 to 12 minutes. Immediately remove from cookie sheet. ABOUT 4 DOZEN.

Rich Date Drops: Substitute ½ cup cut-up dates for the chocolate chips.

MOLDED COOKIES

Two-Way Chocolate Cookies

    1   cup sugar
    ½   cup margarine or butter, softened
    ⅓   cup milk
    2   ounces melted unsweetened chocolate
            (cool)
    1   egg
    1   teaspoon vanilla
    2   cups all-purpose flour*
    ½   teaspoon baking powder
    ½   teaspoon salt
    1   cup chopped pecans

Mix sugar, margarine, milk, chocolate, egg and vanilla in large mixer bowl. Beat in remaining ingredients on low speed, scraping bowl constantly, until soft dough forms. Use half of the dough for Caramelitas (below) and half for Coco-Nut Balls (right).

*If using self-rising flour, omit baking powder and salt.

CARAMELITAS
    ½   chocolate dough (above)
    18 vanilla caramels or candied cherries, cut
            into halves
    1½ cups powdered sugar
    1   ounce melted unsweetened chocolate
            (cool)
    2   tablespoons light corn syrup
    2   to 3 tablespoons hot water

Cover and refrigerate dough at least 1 hour. Heat oven to 400°. Shape dough by rounded teaspoonfuls around caramel halves. Place on ungreased cookie sheet. Bake until set, about 7 minutes; cool. Beat remaining ingredients in small bowl until thickened. Swirl tops of cookies in chocolate mixture.   ABOUT 3 DOZEN.

COCO-NUT BALLS
Heat oven to 400°. Work 2 cups flaked coconut into ½ chocolate dough (left). Shape dough by rounded teaspoonfuls into balls. Roll balls in additional coconut if desired. Place on ungreased cookie sheet. Bake until set, about 7 minutes.   ABOUT 4 DOZEN.

Chocolate Crinkles

    2   cups granulated sugar
    ½   cup vegetable oil
    4   ounces melted unsweetened chocolate
            (cool)
    2   teaspoons vanilla
    4   eggs
    2   cups all-purpose flour*
    2   teaspoons baking powder
    ½   teaspoon salt
    1   cup powdered sugar

Mix granulated sugar, oil, chocolate and vanilla. Mix in eggs, 1 at a time. Stir in flour, baking powder and salt. Cover and refrigerate at least 3 hours.

Heat oven to 350°. Drop dough by teaspoonfuls into powdered sugar; roll around to coat. Shape into balls. Place about 2 inches apart on greased cookie sheet. Bake until almost no indentation remains when touched, 10 to 12 minutes.   ABOUT 6 DOZEN.

*If using self-rising flour, omit baking powder and salt.

Hidden Chocolate Cookies

½ cup granulated sugar
¼ cup packed brown sugar
¼ cup margarine or butter, softened
¼ cup shortening
1 egg
½ teaspoon vanilla
1⅔ cups all-purpose flour *
½ teaspoon baking soda
¼ teaspoon salt
About 30 chocolate mint wafers

Heat oven to 400°. Mix sugars, margarine, shortening, egg and vanilla. Stir in flour, baking soda and salt. Shape about 1 tablespoonful dough around each wafer. Place about 2 inches apart on ungreased cookie sheet. Bake until light brown, 9 to 10 minutes.　ABOUT 2½ DOZEN.

*If using self-rising flour, omit baking soda and salt.

Coconut-Cereal Cookies

½ cup packed brown sugar
¼ cup granulated sugar
¼ cup shortening
1 egg
¼ teaspoon vanilla
1 cup all-purpose flour *
½ teaspoon baking soda
¼ teaspoon salt
1 cup coconut
1 cup whole wheat flake cereal

Heat oven to 375°. Mix sugars, shortening, egg and vanilla. Stir in remaining ingredients. Shape dough by teaspoonfuls into balls. Place on ungreased cookie sheet. Bake until light brown but not set, 7 to 8 minutes.　ABOUT 2½ DOZEN.

*If using self-rising flour, omit baking soda and salt.

Coconut Butter Balls

1 cup margarine or butter, softened
½ cup sugar
2 teaspoons vanilla
2 cups all-purpose flour *
¼ teaspoon salt
About 4 dozen pecan halves
1 egg white
1 tablespoon water
About 1½ cups flaked coconut

Heat oven to 350°. Mix margarine, sugar and vanilla. Stir in flour and salt. (If dough is soft, cover and refrigerate until firm enough to shape.) For each cookie, shape dough around pecan half (cut very large pecan halves in two) to form 1-inch ball. Beat egg white and water with fork. Dip balls into egg white mixture, then into coconut. Place on ungreased cookie sheet. Bake until light brown, 14 to 15 minutes. Store in tightly covered container.　ABOUT 4 DOZEN.

*If using self-rising flour, omit salt.

Snickerdoodles

1½ cups sugar
½ cup margarine or butter, softened
½ cup shortening
2 eggs
2¾ cups all-purpose flour *
2 teaspoons cream of tartar
1 teaspoon baking soda
¼ teaspoon salt
2 tablespoons sugar
2 teaspoons ground cinnamon

Heat oven to 400°. Mix 1½ cups sugar, the margarine, shortening and eggs. Stir in flour, cream of tartar, baking soda and salt. Shape dough by rounded teaspoonfuls into balls. Mix 2 tablespoons sugar and the cinnamon; roll balls in mixture to coat. Place about 2 inches apart on ungreased cookie sheet. Bake until set, 8 to 10 minutes. Immediately remove from cookie sheet.　ABOUT 6 DOZEN.

*If using self-rising flour, omit cream of tartar, baking soda and salt.

Sand Tarts

These fragile, almond-flavored shells of Swedish origin are made in fluted molds.

- ¾ cup sugar
- ¾ cup margarine or butter, softened
- 1 egg white
- 1¾ cups all-purpose flour*
- ⅓ cup finely chopped blanched almonds
- 4 unblanched almonds, finely chopped

Mix sugar, margarine and egg white. Stir in remaining ingredients. Cover and refrigerate at least 2 hours.

Heat oven to 350°. Press dough about ⅛ inch thick on bottom and side of each ungreased *sandbakelse* mold. Place on cookie sheet. Bake 12 to 15 minutes; cool. Gently tap cookies from molds.   ABOUT 3 DOZEN.

*Self-rising flour can be used in this recipe.

Vanilla Crispies

- 1 cup sugar
- 1 cup margarine or butter, softened
- 1 egg
- 2 teaspoons vanilla
- 2 cups all-purpose* or whole wheat flour
- ½ teaspoon baking soda
- ½ teaspoon cream of tartar

Mix sugar, margarine, egg and vanilla. Stir in remaining ingredients. Cover and refrigerate at least 1 hour.

Heat oven to 375°. Shape dough into 1-inch balls. Place about 2 inches apart on ungreased cookie sheet. Flatten with bottom of glass dipped in sugar. Bake until light brown, 8 to 10 minutes. Immediately remove from cookie sheet.   ABOUT 6 DOZEN.

*If using self-rising flour, omit baking soda and cream of tartar.

Cinnamon Crispies: Flatten cookies with bottom of glass dipped in mixture of 1 tablespoon sugar and 1 teaspoon ground cinnamon.

Orange Crispies: Stir in 1 to 2 teaspoons grated orange peel.

Russian Teacakes

- 1 cup margarine or butter, softened
- ½ cup powdered sugar
- 1 teaspoon vanilla
- 2¼ cups all-purpose* or whole wheat flour
- ¼ teaspoon salt
- ¾ cup finely chopped nuts
  Powdered or colored sugar

Heat oven to 400°. Mix margarine, ½ cup powdered sugar and the vanilla. Stir in flour, salt and nuts. Shape dough into 1-inch balls. Place on ungreased cookie sheet. Bake until set but not brown, 8 to 9 minutes. Roll in powdered sugar while warm; cool. Roll in powdered sugar again.   ABOUT 4 DOZEN.

*Do not use self-rising flour in this recipe.

Ambrosia Balls: Substitute 1 cup cookie coconut and 1 tablespoon grated orange peel for the nuts.

Surprise Candy Teacakes: Decrease nuts to ½ cup. Cut 12 vanilla caramels into fourths or cut 1 bar (4 ounces) sweet cooking chocolate into ½-inch squares. Shape dough around pieces of caramel or chocolate to form 1-inch balls.

Sugar Cakes

 2 cups all-purpose flour *
 1 cup margarine or butter, softened
 ¾ cup powdered sugar
 ½ cup half-and-half
1½ teaspoons vanilla
 ½ cup coarsely chopped pecans or walnuts

Mix all ingredients. Cover and refrigerate at least 2 hours.

Heat oven to 350°. Shape dough into 1-inch balls. Place on ungreased cookie sheet. Bake until light brown, about 20 minutes. ABOUT 4 DOZEN.

*Do not use self-rising flour in this recipe.

Holiday Sugar Cookies: Roll tops of balls in colored sugar or nonpareils before baking.

Brazilian Coffee Cookies

 ½ cup granulated sugar
 ½ cup packed brown sugar
 ⅓ cup shortening
 1 egg
 1 tablespoon milk
1½ teaspoons vanilla
1½ cups all-purpose flour *
 2 tablespoons powdered instant coffee
 ½ teaspoon salt
 ¼ teaspoon baking soda
 ¼ teaspoon baking powder

Heat oven to 400°. Mix sugars, shortening, egg, milk and vanilla. Stir in remaining ingredients. Shape dough into 1-inch balls. Place about 2 inches apart on ungreased cookie sheet. Flatten to ⅛-inch thickness with greased fork dipped in sugar (press only in one direction) or with greased bottom of glass dipped in sugar. Bake until light brown, 7 to 8 minutes. ABOUT 3½ DOZEN.

*If using self-rising flour, omit salt, baking soda and baking powder.

Bonbon Cookies

Pictured at right.

 ¾ cup powdered sugar
 ½ cup margarine or butter, softened
 1 tablespoon vanilla
   Few drops food color, if desired
1½ cups all-purpose flour *
 ⅛ teaspoon salt
   Dates, nuts, semisweet chocolate chips, candied cherries or maraschino cherries
   Glaze or Chocolate Glaze (below)

Heat oven to 350°. Mix powdered sugar, margarine, vanilla and food color. Work in flour and salt until dough holds together. (If dough is dry, mix in 1 to 2 tablespoons milk.) For each cookie, shape dough by tablespoonful around date, nut, chocolate chips or cherry to form ball. Place about 1 inch apart on ungreased cookie sheet. Bake until set but not brown, 12 to 15 minutes; cool. Dip tops of cookies into Glaze. Decorate with coconut, nuts, colored sugar, chocolate chips or chocolate shot if desired. ABOUT 2 DOZEN.

*Do not use self-rising flour in this recipe.

GLAZE
Beat 1 cup powdered sugar, 1 tablespoon plus 1½ teaspoons milk and 1 teaspoon vanilla until smooth and of desired consistency. Tint parts of glaze with different food colors if desired.

CHOCOLATE GLAZE
Beat 1 cup powdered sugar, 2 tablespoons milk, 1 ounce melted unsweetened chocolate (cool) and 1 teaspoon vanilla until smooth and of desired consistency.

Brown Sugar Bonbon Cookies: Substitute ½ cup packed brown sugar for the powdered sugar. Omit food color.

Chocolate Bonbon Cookies: Omit food color. Stir 1 ounce melted unsweetened chocolate (cool) into margarine mixture.

Cookies for celebrations—Bonbon Cookies (page 66), Holiday Spritz (page 90), Coconut-Orange Tartlets (page 75) and Almond-Cherry Strips (page 36)

An old-time favorite—Farm-style Oatmeal Cookies (page 82)

When holidays are in season—Heart Cookies (page 33), Pumpkin-shaped Cookies (page 38), Easter Egg Cookies (page 33) and Hamantaschen (page 33)

Roll each piece of dough in colored sugar until it forms a strip about 10 inches long.

On cookie sheet, shape strip into a horseshoe. Lift one end over to cross; repeat with other end.

Pretzel Cookies (page 71)

Pretzel Cookies

Pictured at left.

- 1 **cup sugar**
- 1 **cup margarine or butter, softened**
- ½ **cup milk**
- 1 **egg**
- 1 **teaspoon vanilla**
- 1 **teaspoon almond extract**
- 3½ **cups all-purpose flour***
- 1 **teaspoon baking powder**
- ¼ **teaspoon salt**
  Colored sugar

Mix 1 cup sugar, the margarine, milk, egg, vanilla and almond extract. Stir in flour, baking powder and salt. Cover and refrigerate at least 4 hours.

Heat oven to 375°. Divide dough into 4 equal parts. Divide 1 part into 12 equal pieces (keep remaining dough refrigerated). Sprinkle about 1 teaspoon colored sugar on board. Roll each piece of dough on sugared board into pencil-like strip, about 10 inches long. Twist into pretzel shape on ungreased cookie sheet. Repeat with remaining dough. Bake until delicate golden brown, 10 to 12 minutes.   ABOUT 4 DOZEN.

*If using self-rising flour, omit baking powder and salt.

Glazed Pretzel Cookies: Omit colored sugar; roll strips on floured board. Bake as directed; cool. Beat 1 cup powdered sugar, ½ teaspoon almond extract and about 1 tablespoon milk until smooth and of desired consistency. Tint with few drops food color if desired. Drizzle over cookies.

Cookie-Candies

- 1 **cup margarine or butter, softened**
- ¾ **cup powdered sugar**
- 1 **tablespoon vanilla**
- 2 **cups all-purpose flour***
- ½ **cup oats**
- ¾ **teaspoon salt**
- ¼ **cup semisweet chocolate chips**
- 2 **tablespoons milk**
  Finely chopped pecans, shredded coconut or chocolate shot

Heat oven to 325°. Mix margarine, powdered sugar and vanilla. Stir in flour, oats and salt. Shape dough by teaspoonfuls into balls, crescents, triangles and bars. Place on ungreased cookie sheet. Bake until edges are golden brown, 19 to 20 minutes. (Watch carefully; these cookies are easily overbaked.) Cool.

Heat chocolate chips over low heat until melted. Stir in milk until smooth. Dip tops of cookies into chocolate, then into pecans.   ABOUT 4 DOZEN.

*Do not use self-rising flour in this recipe.

Crisp Pastel Cookies

- ¾ **cup shortening (part margarine or butter, softened)**
- ½ **cup sugar**
- 1 **package (3 ounces) fruit-flavored gelatin**
- 2 **eggs**
- 1 **teaspoon vanilla**
- 2½ **cups all-purpose flour***
- 1 **teaspoon baking powder**
- 1 **teaspoon salt**

Heat oven to 400°. Mix shortening, sugar, gelatin, eggs and vanilla. Stir in remaining ingredients. Shape dough into ¾-inch balls. Place about 3 inches apart on ungreased cookie sheet. Flatten with bottom of glass dipped in sugar. Bake 6 to 8 minutes.   ABOUT 5 DOZEN.

*If using self-rising flour, omit baking powder and salt.

Fortune Cookies

2½ dozen paper fortunes (2½x½ inch)
½ cup all-purpose flour
¼ cup sugar
1 tablespoon cornstarch
  Dash of salt
¼ cup vegetable oil
1 teaspoon almond extract
2 egg whites

Prepare paper fortunes. Heat oven to 300°. Mix flour, sugar, cornstarch and salt. Beat in remaining ingredients until smooth. For each cookie, spoon 1 heaping teaspoonful batter onto well-greased cookie sheet; spread into 3½-inch circle with back of spoon. Bake only 4 cookies at a time; cool cookie sheet and grease well each time. Bake until golden brown, about 10 minutes.

Working quickly, remove 1 cookie at a time with wide spatula; flip into protected hand. (Leave remaining cookies in oven.) Place paper fortune on center of cookie; fold cookie in half. Holding points of folded cookie with both hands, place center of fold over edge of bowl and pull points downward to make a crease across center. Place cookie in ungreased muffin cup so it will hold its shape while cooling. If cookie cools before it is formed, heat in oven about 1 minute. Store in tightly covered container. ABOUT 2 DOZEN.

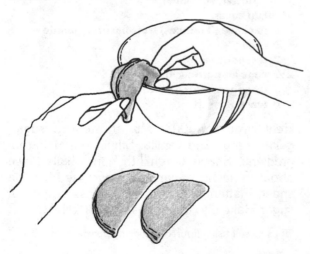

Little Wreaths

Norwegians serve these buttery little cookies, also known as *Berlinerkranzer*, to celebrate Christmas.

1 cup sugar
¾ cup margarine or butter, softened
¾ cup shortening
2 teaspoons grated orange peel
2 eggs
4 cups all-purpose flour*
1 egg white
2 tablespoons sugar
  Red candied cherries
  Green candied citron

Heat oven to 400°. Mix 1 cup sugar, the margarine, shortening, orange peel and eggs. Stir in flour. Shape dough by rounded teaspoonfuls into ropes, about 6 inches long. Form each rope into circle, crossing ends and tucking under. (This shaping method is easier than the traditional method of tying knots.) Place on ungreased cookie sheet. Beat egg white and 2 tablespoons sugar until foamy; brush over tops of cookies. Press bits of candied cherries on center of knot for holly berries; add little jagged leaves cut from citron. Bake until set but not brown, 10 to 12 minutes. Immediately remove from cookie sheet. ABOUT 6 DOZEN.

*Self-rising flour can be used in this recipe.

Marzipan Cookies

  1 **cup margarine or butter, softened**
  ½ **cup sugar**
2½ **cups all-purpose flour***
  ½ **to 1 teaspoon almond extract**
      Food color

Mix margarine and sugar. Stir in flour and almond extract until mixture resembles coarse crumbs. Divide into 3 equal parts. Tint and shape dough as directed below. Place cookies on ungreased cookie sheet. Cover and refrigerate at least 30 minutes.

Heat oven to 300°. Bake until set but not brown, about 30 minutes. ABOUT 4 DOZEN.

*Do not use self-rising flour in this recipe.

APPLES
Mix red or green food color into part of dough. Shape into small balls. Insert small piece of stick cinnamon in top of each for stem end and whole clove in bottom of each for blossom end. Dilute red or green food color with water and brush over apples.

APRICOTS
Mix red and yellow food colors into part of dough. Shape into small balls. Make crease down 1 side of each with wooden pick. Insert whole clove in each for stem end. Dilute red food color with water and brush over apricots.

BANANAS
Mix yellow food color into part of dough. Shape into 3-inch rolls, tapering ends to resemble bananas. Flatten tops slightly to show planes of banana; curve each slightly. Paint on characteristic markings with mixture of red, yellow and blue food colors diluted with water.

GREEN PEAS
Mix green food color into part of dough. Shape into 1½- to 2-inch flat rounds. Divide level teaspoonfuls of dough into 3 or 4 parts; shape each into small ball. Place 3 or 4 small balls in a row down center of each round. Bring dough up and around small balls; pinch edges together to resemble filled pea pods.

ORANGES
Mix red and yellow food colors into part of dough. Shape into small balls. Insert whole clove in each for blossom end. Prick balls with blunt end of wooden pick to resemble texture of orange peel.

PEARS
Mix yellow food color into part of dough. Shape into small balls, then into cone shapes, rounding narrow end of each. Insert small piece of stick cinnamon in narrow end for stem. Dilute red food color with water and brush on "cheeks" of pears.

STRAWBERRIES
Mix red food color into part of dough. Shape into small balls, then into heart shapes (about ¾ inch high). Prick with blunt end of wooden pick for texture. Roll each in red sugar. Insert small piece of green-colored wooden pick or green dough into top of each for stem.

Christmas Stockings

  ½ **cup powdered sugar**
  ½ **cup margarine or butter, softened**
  ½ **cup shortening**
  1 **teaspoon vanilla**
  ½ **teaspoon almond extract**
  ¼ **to ½ teaspoon red or green food color**
2¼ **cups all-purpose flour***
  ½ **teaspoon salt**
      About ¼ cup semisweet chocolate chips
      About 9 candied cherries, each cut into
        fourths
      About ¼ cup broken nuts
      Decorators' Frosting (page 31)

Heat oven to 400°. Mix powdered sugar, margarine, shortening, vanilla, almond extract and food color. Stir in flour and salt. Shape dough by level tablespoonfuls into rectangles, about 3x1½ inches. (If dough seems dry, stir in ½ to 1 teaspoon milk.)

Place 2 chocolate chips, 1 cherry piece and 2 pieces of nuts lengthwise down center of each rectangle. Shape dough around "surprises" into 3-inch roll. Place on ungreased cookie sheet; flatten slightly and curve end to form foot of stocking. Bake until set, 10 to 12 minutes; cool. Frost tops and toes with Decorators' Frosting. ABOUT 3 DOZEN.

*Do not use self-rising flour in this recipe.

Candy Cane Cookies

    1 cup powdered sugar
    ½ cup margarine or butter, softened
    ½ cup shortening
    1 egg
    1½ teaspoons almond extract
    1 teaspoon vanilla
    2½ cups all-purpose flour*
    1 teaspoon salt
    ½ teaspoon red food color
    ½ cup crushed peppermint candy
    ½ cup granulated sugar

Heat oven to 375°. Mix powdered sugar, margarine, shortening, egg, almond extract and vanilla. Stir in flour and salt. Divide dough into halves. Tint 1 half with food color. For each candy cane, shape 1 teaspoon dough from each part into 4-inch rope. For smooth, even strips, roll back and forth on lightly floured board. Place 1 red and 1 white strip side by side; press together lightly and twist. Complete cookies 1 at a time. Place on ungreased cookie sheet. Curve top down to form handle of cane. Bake until set and very light brown, about 9 minutes. Mix candy and granulated sugar; immediately sprinkle over cookies. Remove from cookie sheet.   ABOUT 4 DOZEN.

*If using self-rising flour, omit salt.

Peppermint Candy Canes: Substitute peppermint extract for the almond extract.

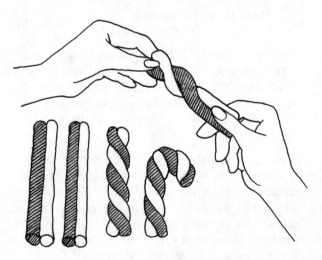

Greek Easter Cookies

For a more authentic Greek cookie, omit ground cloves and place a whole clove in the center of each cookie before baking.

    1 cup margarine or butter, softened
    ⅓ cup granulated sugar
    2 egg yolks
    1 teaspoon vanilla
    ½ teaspoon brandy flavoring, if desired
    2 cups all-purpose flour*
    1 teaspoon baking powder
    1 teaspoon ground cloves
       Powdered sugar

Heat oven to 350°. Mix margarine, granulated sugar, egg yolks, vanilla and brandy flavoring. Stir in flour, baking powder and cloves. Shape dough into ¾-inch balls or 2-inch-long crescents. Place on ungreased cookie sheet. Bake until set but not brown, 8 to 10 minutes. Cool 2 minutes; remove from cookie sheet. Cool completely; roll in powdered sugar. ABOUT 6½ DOZEN.

*If using self-rising flour, omit baking powder.

Cherry-topped Cookies

    1 cup all-purpose flour*
    ½ cup sugar
    ⅓ cup shortening
    1 egg
    1 tablespoon plus 1½ teaspoons milk
    ½ teaspoon baking powder
    ½ teaspoon vanilla
    ¼ teaspoon baking soda
    ¼ teaspoon salt
    ½ cup raisins or cut-up dates
    ½ cup chopped nuts
    1½ cups whole wheat flake cereal, crushed
       Candied or maraschino cherries

Heat oven to 375°. Mix flour, sugar, shortening, egg, milk, baking powder, vanilla, baking soda and salt. Stir in raisins and nuts. Drop dough by teaspoonfuls into cereal; roll around to coat. Place balls about 2 inches apart on greased cookie sheet. Top each with piece of cherry. Bake 10 to 12 minutes.   ABOUT 3 DOZEN.

*If using self-rising flour, omit baking powder, baking soda and salt.

Coconut-Orange Tartlets

Pictured on page 67.

½ cup margarine or butter
1 cup all-purpose flour*
¼ cup sugar
½ teaspoon salt
1 egg
  Coconut-Orange Filling (below)

Cut margarine into flour, sugar and salt thoroughly. Beat egg slightly; pour over flour mixture. Mix with fork until flour is moistened. Gather dough into ball. Wrap and refrigerate until firm, about 4 hours.

Heat oven to 375°. For each tart, press about 1 teaspoon dough about ⅛ inch thick on bottom and side of each ungreased 2x½-inch tartlet pan or 1¾x1-inch muffin cup. Fill each tart with about 1 teaspoon Coconut-Orange Filling. Place on cookie sheet. Bake until filling is golden brown, about 12 minutes; cool slightly. Gently tap tartlets from pans.   ABOUT 3½ DOZEN.

*Do not use self-rising flour in this recipe.

COCONUT-ORANGE FILLING

Mix 1 egg, slightly beaten, 1 can (4 ounces) flaked coconut, ⅔ cup sugar and ½ teaspoon grated orange or lemon peel.

Lemon-Ginger Crinkles

1 cup packed brown sugar
½ cup shortening
1 egg
1 tablespoon grated lemon peel
1½ cups all-purpose flour*
½ teaspoon baking soda
½ teaspoon cream of tartar
¼ teaspoon salt
¼ teaspoon ground ginger
  Granulated sugar

Heat oven to 350°. Mix brown sugar, shortening, egg and lemon peel. Stir in flour, baking soda, cream of tartar, salt and ginger. Shape dough into 1-inch balls; dip tops in granulated sugar. Place on ungreased cookie sheet. Bake until almost no indentation remains when touched, 10 to 11 minutes.   ABOUT 4 DOZEN.

*If using self-rising flour, omit baking soda and salt.

Lemon Snowdrops

1 cup margarine or butter, softened
½ cup powdered sugar
1 teaspoon lemon extract
2 cups all-purpose flour*
¼ teaspoon salt
  Lemon Butter Filling (below)
  Powdered sugar

Heat oven to 400°. Mix margarine, ½ cup powdered sugar and the lemon extract. Stir in flour and salt. (If dough is soft, cover and refrigerate until firm enough to shape, 1 to 2 hours.) Shape dough into 1-inch balls. Place about 1 inch apart on ungreased cookie sheet; flatten slightly. Bake until edges are light brown, 8 to 10 minutes. Immediately remove from cookie sheet; cool. Put cookies together in pairs with Lemon Butter Filling. Roll in powdered sugar.   ABOUT 2 DOZEN.

*If using self-rising flour, omit salt.

LEMON BUTTER FILLING

¼ cup sugar
2¼ teaspoons cornstarch
  Dash of salt
¼ cup water
1 tablespoon margarine or butter
1 teaspoon grated lemon peel
1 tablespoon plus 1½ teaspoons lemon juice
2 drops yellow food color

Mix sugar, cornstarch and salt in 1-quart saucepan. Stir in remaining ingredients. Cook over medium heat, stirring constantly, until mixture thickens and boils. Boil and stir 1 minute; cool.

Date-Oatmeal Cookies

    1 cup packed brown sugar
    ½ cup shortening
    ¼ cup margarine or butter, softened
    2 eggs
    3 tablespoons milk
    1 teaspoon vanilla
    2 cups all-purpose flour*
    ¾ teaspoon baking soda
    1 teaspoon salt
    2 cups oats
    1½ cups cut-up dates
    ¾ cup chopped nuts

Mix brown sugar, shortening, margarine, eggs, milk and vanilla. Stir in remaining ingredients. Cover and refrigerate at least 2 hours.

Heat oven to 375°. Shape dough into 1¼-inch balls. Place about 3 inches apart on ungreased cookie sheet. Flatten to ¼-inch thickness with bottom of glass dipped in flour. Bake until light brown, 9 to 10 minutes.   ABOUT 4 DOZEN.

*If using self-rising flour, omit baking soda and salt.

Raisin Crisscross Cookies

    ¾ cup sugar
    ¼ cup margarine or butter, softened
    ¼ cup shortening
    1 egg
    ½ teaspoon lemon extract
    1¾ cups all-purpose flour*
    ¾ teaspoon cream of tartar
    ¾ teaspoon baking soda
    ¼ teaspoon salt
    1 cup raisins

Heat oven to 400°. Mix sugar, margarine, shortening, egg and lemon extract. Stir in remaining ingredients. Shape dough by rounded teaspoonfuls into balls. Place about 3 inches apart on ungreased cookie sheet. Flatten in crisscross pattern with fork dipped in flour. Bake until light brown, 8 to 10 minutes.   ABOUT 3 DOZEN.

*If using self-rising flour, omit cream of tartar, baking soda and salt.

Chocolate Crisscross Cookies: Substitute ½ cup semisweet chocolate chips for the raisins.

Jam Bites

    1½ cups powdered sugar
    1 cup margarine or butter, softened
    1 egg
    1 teaspoon vanilla
    ½ teaspoon almond extract
    2½ cups all-purpose flour*
    1 teaspoon baking soda
    1 teaspoon cream of tartar
    ½ cup jam
       Glaze (below)

Mix powdered sugar, margarine, egg, vanilla and almond extract. Stir in flour, baking soda and cream of tartar. (If dough is soft, cover and refrigerate at least 1 hour.)

Heat oven to 375°. Divide dough into 12 equal parts. Shape each part into strip, 8x1½ inches, on lightly greased cookie sheet. Make indentation lengthwise down center of each strip with handle of wooden spoon; spread 1 teaspoon jam in each. Bake about 10 minutes. Cool 2 minutes; cut strips at an angle into 1-inch slices. Remove from cookie sheet; cool. Drizzle with Glaze.   8 DOZEN.

*If using self-rising flour, omit baking soda and cream of tartar.

GLAZE
Beat 2 cups powdered sugar and 2 tablespoons plus 1 teaspoon milk until smooth and of desired consistency.

Thumbprint Cookies

Pictured on page 79.

¼ cup packed brown sugar
¼ cup margarine or butter, softened
¼ cup shortening
1 egg, separated
½ teaspoon vanilla
1 cup all-purpose* or whole wheat flour
¼ teaspoon salt
¾ cup finely chopped nuts
  Jelly

Heat oven to 350°. Mix brown sugar, margarine, shortening, egg yolk and vanilla. Stir in flour and salt. Shape dough into 1-inch balls. Beat egg white slightly. Dip balls into egg white; roll in nuts. Place about 1 inch apart on ungreased cookie sheet; press thumb deeply in center of each. Bake until light brown, about 10 minutes. Immediately remove from cookie sheet; cool. Fill thumbprints with jelly.   ABOUT 3 DOZEN.

*If using self-rising flour, omit salt.

Gingersnaps

1 cup sugar
¾ cup shortening
¼ cup dark molasses
1 egg
2¼ cups all-purpose flour*
1½ teaspoons baking soda
1 tablespoon ground ginger
1 teaspoon ground cinnamon
¼ teaspoon salt
  Sugar

Mix 1 cup sugar, the shortening, molasses and egg. Stir in flour, baking soda, ginger, cinnamon and salt. Cover and refrigerate at least 1 hour.

Heat oven to 375°. Shape dough by rounded teaspoonfuls into balls; dip tops in sugar. Place balls, sugared sides up, about 3 inches apart on lightly greased cookie sheet. Bake until edges are set (centers will be soft), 10 to 12 minutes. Immediately remove from cookie sheet.   ABOUT 4 DOZEN.

*If using self-rising flour, omit baking soda and salt.

Molasses Cookies

These small, hard German cookies, also called Peppernuts, or *Pfeffernüsse*, have a mild anise flavor.

¾ cup packed brown sugar
½ cup shortening
½ cup molasses
1 egg
1 tablespoon hot water
3 drops anise oil
3⅓ cups all-purpose flour*
½ teaspoon baking soda
½ teaspoon ground cinnamon
½ teaspoon ground cloves
¼ teaspoon salt
⅛ teaspoon white pepper

Heat oven to 350°. Mix brown sugar, shortening, molasses, egg, water and anise oil. Stir in remaining ingredients. Knead dough until right consistency for molding. Shape dough into ¾-inch balls. Place about 1 inch apart on ungreased cookie sheet. Bake until bottoms are golden brown, about 12 minutes.   ABOUT 8 DOZEN.

*If using self-rising flour, omit baking soda and salt.

Honey Drops

1 cup packed brown sugar
½ cup margarine or butter, softened
½ cup shortening
⅓ cup honey
2 eggs
1 teaspoon vanilla
3½ cups all-purpose flour*
2 teaspoons baking soda
  Apricot jam

Heat oven to 350°. Mix brown sugar, margarine, shortening, honey, eggs and vanilla. Stir in flour and baking soda. Shape dough into 1¼-inch balls. Place on ungreased cookie sheet. Bake until almost no indentation remains when touched, about 11 minutes; cool. Put cookies together in pairs with jam.   ABOUT 2 DOZEN.

*If using self-rising flour, omit baking soda.

Filbert Cookies

¾ cup sugar
½ cup margarine or butter, softened
½ cup shortening
1 egg
2½ cups all-purpose flour*
1½ teaspoons vanilla
½ teaspoon baking powder
⅛ teaspoon salt
2 to 3 ounces filberts
　 Glaze (below)
　 Sugar

Heat oven to 375°. Mix ¾ cup sugar, the margarine, shortening and egg. Stir in flour, vanilla, baking powder and salt. Shape dough by teaspoonfuls around filberts to form balls. Place about 1 inch apart on ungreased cookie sheet. Bake until delicate brown, 12 to 15 minutes; cool. Dip tops of cookies into Glaze, then into sugar. ABOUT 7 DOZEN.

*If using self-rising flour, omit baking powder and salt.

GLAZE
Beat 2 cups powdered sugar, 3 tablespoons water and 1 teaspoon almond extract until smooth and of desired consistency.

Peanut Butter Crunchies

1 cup packed brown sugar
1 cup margarine or butter, softened
⅔ cup crunchy peanut butter
1 egg
1 teaspoon vanilla
1⅓ cups all-purpose flour*
½ teaspoon baking soda
¼ teaspoon salt
¾ cup crushed whole wheat flake cereal

Mix brown sugar, margarine, peanut butter, egg and vanilla. Stir in flour, baking soda and salt. Cover and refrigerate at least 2 hours.

Heat oven to 350°. Shape dough into 1-inch balls; roll in cereal. Place about 2 inches apart on ungreased cookie sheet. Bake until almost no indentation remains when touched, 12 to 13 minutes. ABOUT 4½ DOZEN.

*If using self-rising flour, omit baking soda and salt.

Peanut Butter Cookies

Pictured at right.

½ cup granulated sugar
½ cup packed brown sugar
¼ cup margarine or butter, softened
¼ cup shortening
½ cup peanut butter
1 egg
1¼ cups all-purpose* or whole
　　 wheat flour
¾ teaspoon baking soda
½ teaspoon baking powder
¼ teaspoon salt

Mix sugars, margarine, shortening, peanut butter and egg. Stir in remaining ingredients. Cover and refrigerate at least 3 hours.

Heat oven to 375°. Shape dough into 1¼-inch balls. Place about 3 inches apart on ungreased cookie sheet. Flatten in crisscross pattern with fork dipped in flour. Bake until light brown, 9 to 10 minutes. Cool 2 minutes; remove from cookie sheet. ABOUT 3 DOZEN.

*If using self-rising flour, omit baking soda, baking powder and salt.

Invisible-Mint Cookies: For each cookie, shape 1 level tablespoonful dough around chocolate mint wafer. Place on lightly greased cookie sheet. Sprinkle tops with finely chopped peanuts or chocolate shot. Bake until set but not hard, 10 to 12 minutes.

Peanut Butter and Jelly Cookies: Shape dough into 1-inch balls. Roll balls in ½ cup finely chopped peanuts. Place about 3 inches apart on lightly greased cookie sheet; press thumb deeply in center of each. Bake until set but not hard, 10 to 12 minutes. Fill thumbprints with jam or jelly. ABOUT 3½ DOZEN.

Peanut Butter Sandwich Cookies: Shape dough into ¾-inch balls. Place about 2 inches apart on lightly greased cookie sheet. Do not flatten. Bake until set but not hard, about 10 minutes; cool. Put cookies together in pairs with jelly or jam. ABOUT 2 DOZEN.

Cookies made with whole wheat flour—Thumbprint Cookies (page 77), Chocolate Chip Cookies (page 46), Peanut Butter Cookies (page 78) and Butterscotch Brownies (page 14)

Refrigerate these cookie doughs in advance; slice and bake when you're ready—Date-Nut Pinwheels (page 87), Molasses-Ginger Slices (page 88) and Candied Fruit Slices (page 86)

Quick Peanut Butter Cookies

The Quick Peanut Butter Stars variation is a sure-fire party favorite. *Pictured on page 27.*

1 cup peanut butter
½ cup granulated sugar
½ cup packed brown sugar
¼ cup shortening
⅓ cup water
2 cups buttermilk baking mix

Heat oven to 400°. Mix peanut butter, sugars, shortening and water. Stir in baking mix. Shape dough by rounded teaspoonfuls into balls. Place on ungreased cookie sheet. Flatten cookies in crisscross pattern with fork dipped in flour. Bake 5 to 7 minutes. Cool slightly; remove from cookie sheet. ABOUT 4 DOZEN.

Quick Coconut-Peanut Butter Cookies: Mix in 1 cup shredded coconut before stirring in baking mix.

Quick Double Peanut Cookies: Mix in 1 cup chopped peanuts before stirring in baking mix.

Quick Orange-Peanut Butter Cookies: Substitute orange juice for the water. Mix in 2 teaspoons grated orange peel before stirring in baking mix.

Quick Peanut Butter-Chip Cookies: Mix in 1 package (6 ounces) semisweet chocolate chips before stirring in baking mix. Bake until light brown, 8 to 10 minutes.

Quick Peanut Butter Stars: Roll balls in sugar. Place about 2 inches apart on cookie sheet; do not flatten. Bake until edges are light brown, 8 to 10 minutes. Immediately press 1 milk chocolate candy star firmly in each cookie. Cool slightly; remove from cookie sheet. Cool cookies completely.

Pecan Rounds

1 cup sugar
¼ cup margarine or butter, softened
¼ cup shortening
1 egg, separated
3 tablespoons milk
1 teaspoon vanilla
1½ cups all-purpose flour *
¾ teaspoon salt
½ cup finely chopped pecans

Heat oven to 375°. Mix sugar, margarine, shortening, egg yolk, milk and vanilla. Stir in flour and salt. Shape dough into 1-inch balls. Place on ungreased cookie sheet. Flatten to ¹⁄₁₆-inch thickness with greased bottom of glass dipped in sugar. Beat egg white slightly; brush over cookies. Sprinkle with pecans. Bake until very light brown, 8 to 9 minutes. ABOUT 3½ DOZEN.

*If using self-rising flour, omit salt.

Pecan Spice Cookies

1¼ cups packed brown sugar
¼ cup margarine or butter, softened
¼ cup shortening
1 egg
1¾ cups all-purpose flour *
2 teaspoons baking powder
½ teaspoon salt
½ teaspoon ground ginger
½ teaspoon ground cinnamon
½ teaspoon ground cloves
½ teaspoon ground nutmeg
⅓ cup chopped pecans
About 4 dozen pecan halves

Heat oven to 375°. Mix brown sugar, margarine, shortening and egg. Stir in remaining ingredients except pecan halves. Shape dough into 1-inch balls. Place about 2 inches apart on ungreased cookie sheet. Place 1 pecan half on each ball, flattening dough slightly. Bake until light brown, 10 to 11 minutes. Store in tightly covered container. ABOUT 4 DOZEN.

*If using self-rising flour, omit baking powder and salt.

Farm-style Oatmeal Cookies

Pictured on page 68.

      2 cups packed brown sugar
      1 cup lard or shortening
      ½ cup buttermilk
      1 teaspoon vanilla
      4 cups quick-cooking oats
    1¾ cups all-purpose* or whole wheat flour
      1 teaspoon baking soda
      ¾ teaspoon salt

Heat oven to 375°. Mix brown sugar, lard, buttermilk and vanilla. Stir in remaining ingredients. Shape dough into 1-inch balls. Place about 3 inches apart on ungreased cookie sheet. Flatten with bottom of glass dipped in water. Bake until golden brown, 8 to 10 minutes. Immediately remove from cookie sheet.   ABOUT 7 DOZEN.

*If using self-rising flour, omit baking soda and salt.

V.G.

✓Oatmeal-Cinnamon Cookies

      1 cup sugar
      ½ cup margarine or butter, softened
      ½ cup shortening
      2 eggs
      1 teaspoon vanilla
    1¾ cups all-purpose flour*
      1 cup oats
      ½ cup raisins
      1 teaspoon baking soda
      ½ teaspoon salt
      ½ teaspoon ground cinnamon

Heat oven to 375°. Mix sugar, margarine, shortening, eggs and vanilla. Stir in remaining ingredients. Shape dough into 1-inch balls. Place about 2 inches apart on ungreased cookie sheet. Flatten with greased bottom of glass dipped in sugar. Bake until light brown, 10 to 11 minutes.   ABOUT 3½ DOZEN.

*If using self-rising flour, omit baking soda and salt.

Corn Puff Crisps

      ½ cup granulated sugar
      ½ cup packed brown sugar
      ½ cup peanut butter
      ¼ cup margarine or butter, softened
      ¼ cup shortening
      1 egg
      ½ teaspoon baking soda
      ½ teaspoon baking powder
      4 cups corn puff cereal
      1 package (6 ounces) semisweet chocolate chips

Heat oven to 325°. Mix sugars, peanut butter, margarine, shortening, egg, baking soda and baking powder. Stir in cereal and chocolate chips. Shape dough by rounded tablespoonfuls into balls. Place about 2 inches apart on ungreased cookie sheet. Bake until golden, 10 to 12 minutes. Cool 5 minutes; remove from cookie sheet.   ABOUT 3½ DOZEN.

Butterscotch Corn Puff Crisps: Substitute butterscotch chips for the chocolate chips.

Coconut Corn Puff Crisps: Substitute 1 cup coconut for the chocolate chips.

Nutty Corn Puff Crisps: Substitute 1 cup nuts for the chocolate chips.

Raisin Corn Puff Crisps: Substitute 1 cup raisins for the chocolate chips.

Refrigerator, Pressed & Fried Cookies

Chocolate Cookie Slices

Pictured on page 18.

1½ cups powdered sugar
1¼ cups margarine or butter, softened
1 egg
3 cups all-purpose flour*
½ cup cocoa
¼ teaspoon salt
1½ cups finely chopped pecans
   Fudge Frosting (right), if desired

Mix powdered sugar, margarine and egg. Stir in flour, cocoa and salt. Cover and refrigerate 1 hour.

Divide into halves. Shape each half into roll, about 1½ inches in diameter. Roll in pecans. Wrap and refrigerate at least 8 hours but no longer than 6 weeks.

Heat oven to 400°. Cut rolls into ⅛-inch slices. (If dough crumbles while cutting, let warm slightly.) Place about 1 inch apart on ungreased cookie sheet. Bake about 8 minutes. Immediately remove from cookie sheet; cool. Frost with Fudge Frosting.   ABOUT 8 DOZEN.

*Do not use self-rising flour in this recipe.

FUDGE FROSTING
1 cup sugar
⅓ cup milk
¼ cup shortening
2 squares (1 ounce each) unsweetened chocolate
¼ teaspoon salt
1 teaspoon vanilla

Heat sugar, milk, shortening, chocolate and salt to rolling boil, stirring occasionally. Boil 1 minute without stirring. Place pan in bowl of ice and water. Beat until thick and cold; stir in vanilla.

Two-tone Pinwheels: Omit ½ cup cocoa and the pecans. After dough is mixed, divide into halves. Stir ¼ cup cocoa into 1 half. Cover and refrigerate 1 hour. Roll plain dough into rectangle, about 16x9 inches, on lightly floured board. Repeat with chocolate dough; place on plain dough. Roll doughs together to ³⁄₁₆-inch thickness. Roll up tightly, beginning at long side. Wrap and refrigerate. Continue as directed. Omit frosting.

Ribbon Bar Cookies: Omit ½ cup cocoa. After dough is mixed, divide into halves. Stir ¼ cup cocoa into 1 half. Cover and refrigerate 1 hour. Shape each half into 2 strips, each about 2½ inches wide, on very lightly floured board. Layer strips, alternating colors; press together. Wrap and refrigerate. Continue as directed. Omit frosting.   ABOUT 5½ DOZEN.

Chocolate-Granola Slices

    1 cup packed brown sugar
    ½ cup shortening
    1 egg
    1 teaspoon vanilla
    ½ teaspoon almond extract
    1½ cups granola, crushed
    1 cup all-purpose flour
    2 ounces melted unsweetened chocolate
        (cool)
    ½ teaspoon baking soda
    ½ teaspoon salt
    ½ cup chopped nuts

Mix brown sugar, shortening, egg, vanilla and almond extract. Stir in remaining ingredients. Shape into roll, about 1½ inches in diameter. Wrap and refrigerate at least 4 hours.

Heat oven to 350°. Cut roll into ¼-inch slices. (If dough crumbles while cutting, let warm slightly.) Place about 1 inch apart on ungreased cookie sheet. Bake until set, 10 to 12 minutes. Immediately remove from cookie sheet.   ABOUT 4 DOZEN.

Chocolate-Granola Drops: Drop dough by rounded teaspoonfuls about 2 inches apart onto ungreased cookie sheet. Bake 10 to 12 minutes.   ABOUT 4½ DOZEN.

Brownie Refrigerator Cookies

Mix 1 package (15 ounces) fudge brownie mix, 1 egg, ¼ cup vegetable oil and ½ cup finely chopped walnuts. Shape into roll, about 2 inches in diameter. Wrap and refrigerate until firm, about 1 hour.

Heat oven to 375°. Cut roll into ⅛-inch slices. Place on ungreased cookie sheet. Bake 6 to 8 minutes. Immediately remove from cookie sheet.   ABOUT 4 DOZEN.

Orange Brownie Slices: Mix in grated peel of 1 orange. Frost with Orange-Lemon Frosting (page 16).

Rainbow Brownie Slices: Sprinkle tops of cookies with multicolored decorators' candies before baking.

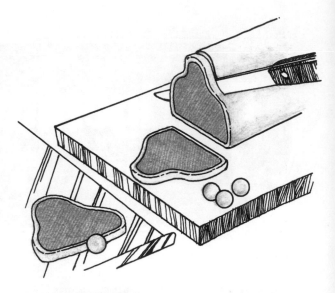

Cookie Bells

    ½ cup sugar
    ¼ cup margarine or butter, softened
    ¼ cup shortening
    1 egg
    1 teaspoon vanilla
    1½ cups all-purpose flour*
    ½ teaspoon salt
    ¼ teaspoon baking soda
      Red or green food color

Mix sugar, margarine, shortening, egg and vanilla. Stir in flour, salt and baking soda. Stir food color into ⅔ of the dough. Shape into roll, about 1½ inches in diameter. Form bell shape by pressing top of roll together and leaving lower half flared and curved. Refrigerate at least 1 hour.

Reserve ¼ cup of the plain dough for clappers. Roll remaining plain dough into rectangle, about 10x4 inches, on waxed paper. Wrap around bell-shaped roll; press together. Refrigerate at least 8 hours.

Heat oven to 375°. Cut roll into ⅛-inch slices. Place on ungreased cookie sheet. Place tiny ball of reserved dough at bottom of each bell for clapper. Bake until edges are light brown, 7 to 8 minutes.   ABOUT 4½ DOZEN.

*If using self-rising flour, omit salt and baking soda.

Christmas Balls: Do not shape dough into bell. Wrap with all of plain dough; roll in colored shot.

Vanilla Cookie Slices

1 cup sugar
1 cup margarine or butter, softened
2 eggs
1½ teaspoons vanilla
3 cups all-purpose flour *
1 teaspoon salt
½ teaspoon baking soda

Mix sugar, margarine, eggs and vanilla. Stir in remaining ingredients. Divide into 3 equal parts. Shape each part into roll, about 1½ inches in diameter. Wrap and refrigerate at least 4 hours but no longer than 6 weeks.

Heat oven to 400°. Cut rolls into ⅛-inch slices. Place about 1 inch apart on ungreased cookie sheet. Bake 8 to 10 minutes. Immediately remove from cookie sheet.   ABOUT 7 DOZEN.

*If using self-rising flour, omit salt.

Butterscotch Slices: Substitute packed brown sugar for the granulated sugar.

Christmas Trees: Divide dough into halves. Shape into 3 rolls, each 14 inches long, using ½ of the dough for the largest roll, ⅔ of the second half for the medium roll and the remaining dough for the smallest roll. Coat rolls with green sugar. Wrap and refrigerate. Heat oven to 400°. Cut each roll into ¼-inch slices. Place about 1 inch apart on ungreased cookie sheet. Bake until edges are delicate brown, 8 to 10 minutes; cool. Stack 3 slices, from largest to smallest, spreading Easy Frosting (page 24) between each. Top each tree with red cinnamon candy dipped in frosting.   ABOUT 4½ DOZEN.

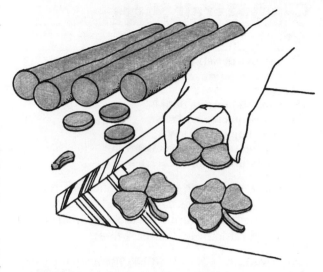

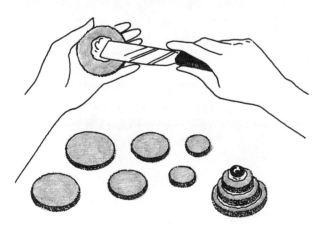

Shamrocks: Tint dough with green food color. Divide into 4 equal parts. Shape each part into roll, about 1 inch in diameter. Coat rolls with green sugar. Wrap and refrigerate. Heat oven to 400°. Cut rolls into ⅛-inch slices. For each cookie, place 3 slices, with sides touching, on ungreased cookie sheet; press sides together; attach stem cut from another slice. Bake about 7 minutes.   ABOUT 6 DOZEN.

Cinnamon Slices: Substitute ½ cup packed brown sugar for ½ cup of the granulated sugar and 1 tablespoon ground cinnamon for the vanilla.

Cookie Tarts: Spoon 1 teaspoon jelly or preserves onto half of the slices; top with remaining slices. Seal edges. Cut slits in tops so filling shows.   3½ DOZEN.

Orange-Almond Slices: Mix in 1 tablespoon grated orange peel with the margarine and ½ cup cut-up blanched almonds with the flour.

Peanut Butter Slices: Substitute packed dark brown sugar for the granulated sugar and ½ cup crunchy peanut butter for ½ cup of the softened margarine.

Walnut Slices: Stir in ½ cup chopped black walnuts.

Whole Wheat Slices: Substitute whole wheat flour for the all-purpose flour.

Candied Fruit Slices

Pictured on page 80.

>   1 cup powdered sugar
>   1 cup margarine or butter, softened
>   1 egg
> 2¼ cups all-purpose flour*
>   ¼ teaspoon cream of tartar
>   ½ cup chopped pecans
>   ½ cup cut-up mixed candied fruit
>   1 cup whole candied cherries

Mix powdered sugar, margarine and egg. Mix in remaining ingredients. Divide into halves. Shape each half into roll, about 1½ inches in diameter. Wrap and refrigerate at least 4 hours.

Heat oven to 375°. Cut rolls into ⅛-inch slices. Place about 1 inch apart on ungreased cookie sheet. Bake until set, about 8 minutes. Immediately remove from cookie sheet.   ABOUT 6 DOZEN.

*Self-rising flour can be used in this recipe.

Filled Cookie Slices

>   ¼ cup granulated sugar
>   ¼ cup packed brown sugar
>   ¼ cup margarine or butter, softened
>   ¼ cup shortening
>   1 egg
> 1¼ cups all-purpose flour*
>   ½ teaspoon salt
>   ¼ teaspoon baking soda
>   Fruit Filling or Mincemeat Filling
>   (right)

Mix sugars, margarine, shortening and egg. Stir in flour, salt and baking soda (dough will be very soft). Divide into halves. Shape each half into roll, about 1½ inches in diameter. Wrap and refrigerate at least 2 hours.

Heat oven to 400°. Cut 1 roll into ⅛-inch slices (keep remaining roll refrigerated). Place on ungreased cookie sheet. Spoon about ½ teaspoon Fruit Filling onto each slice. Cut remaining roll into ⅛-inch slices; top filled slices with remaining slices. Bake until light brown, 7 to 9 minutes. ABOUT 3 DOZEN.

*If using self-rising flour, omit salt and decrease baking soda to ⅛ teaspoon.

FRUIT FILLING

Cook ¼ cup cut-up dates, dried apricots, figs or whole raisins, 2 tablespoons sugar and 2 tablespoons water over medium heat, stirring constantly, until thickened, about 5 minutes; remove from heat. Stir in ¼ cup chopped nuts.

MINCEMEAT FILLING

Mix ¼ cup prepared mincemeat, 2 tablespoons chopped nuts and 1 tablespoon chopped maraschino cherries.

Fruit Slice Cookies

>   1 cup granulated sugar
>   1 cup margarine or butter, softened
>   2 eggs
> 1½ teaspoons vanilla
>   3 cups all-purpose flour*
>   1 teaspoon salt
>   Yellow, green and red food colors
> 1½ teaspoons grated lemon peel
> 1½ teaspoons grated lime peel
> 1½ teaspoons grated orange peel
>   Yellow, green and orange sugars

Mix sugar, margarine, eggs and vanilla. Stir in flour and salt. Divide into 4 equal parts. Mix few drops yellow food color and the lemon peel into 1 part. Mix few drops green food color and the lime peel into another part. Mix few drops each red and yellow food color and the orange peel into another part. Leave remaining part plain. (If necessary, work in food color and peel with hands.) Cover and refrigerate 1 hour.

Shape each part colored dough into roll, about 2 inches in diameter. Divide plain dough into 3 equal parts. Roll each part into rectangle, about 6x4 inches. Wrap rectangle around each roll of colored dough; press together. Roll in matching colored sugar. Wrap and refrigerate at least 4 hours.

Heat oven to 400°. Cut rolls into ⅛-inch slices; cut each slice into halves. Place on ungreased cookie sheet. Bake 6 to 8 minutes. Immediately remove from cookie sheet.   ABOUT 10 DOZEN.

*Do not use self-rising flour in this recipe.

Date-Nut Pinwheels

Pictured on page 80.

12 ounces pitted dates, cut up
⅓ cup granulated sugar
⅓ cup water
½ cup chopped nuts
1 cup packed brown sugar
¼ cup margarine or butter, softened
¼ cup shortening
1 egg
½ teaspoon vanilla
1¾ cups all-purpose flour*
¼ teaspoon salt

Cook dates, granulated sugar and water in saucepan, stirring constantly, until slightly thickened; remove from heat. Stir in nuts; cool.

Mix brown sugar, margarine, shortening, egg and vanilla until smooth. Stir in flour and salt. Divide into halves. Roll each half into rectangle, about 11x7 inches, on waxed paper. Spread half of the date-nut filling over each rectangle. Roll up tightly, beginning at 11-inch side. Pinch edge of dough to seal well. Wrap and refrigerate at least 4 hours but no longer than 6 weeks.

Heat oven to 400°. Cut rolls into ¼-inch slices. Place about 1 inch apart on ungreased cookie sheet. Bake until light brown, about 10 minutes. Immediately remove from cookie sheet.   ABOUT 5 DOZEN.

*If using self-rising flour, omit salt.

Caramel-Nut Cookies: Omit date-nut filling. Stir in 1 cup finely chopped nuts with the flour. Shape each half into roll, about 2 inches in diameter. Wrap and refrigerate at least 4 hours.

Orange-Pecan Cookies: Omit date-nut filling. Mix in 1 tablespoon grated orange peel with the shortening. Stir in ½ cup chopped pecans with the flour. Shape each half into roll, about 2 inches in diameter. Wrap and refrigerate at least 4 hours.

Neapolitan Cookie Slices

1 cup margarine or butter, softened
½ cup sugar
1 egg
1 teaspoon vanilla
2¼ cups all-purpose flour*
½ teaspoon salt
1 ounce melted unsweetened chocolate (cool)
¼ cup chopped walnuts
2 tablespoons finely chopped maraschino cherries

Line loaf pan, 9x5x3 inches, with aluminum foil. Mix margarine, sugar, egg and vanilla. Stir in flour and salt. Divide into thirds. Stir chocolate and walnuts into 1 third. Stir cherries into another third. Leave remaining third plain. Spread plain dough in pan. Top with chocolate dough, then cherry dough. Cover and refrigerate at least 2 hours but no longer than 6 weeks.

Heat oven to 375°. Remove dough from pan; remove foil. Cut dough into ¼-inch slices; cut each slice into halves. Place about 1 inch apart on ungreased cookie sheet. Bake until light brown, about 10 minutes. Immediately remove from cookie sheet.   ABOUT 6½ DOZEN.

*Do not use self-rising flour in this recipe.

Rich Pecan Slices

1 cup powdered sugar
1 cup margarine or butter, softened
1 teaspoon vanilla or almond extract
2½ cups all-purpose flour*
¼ teaspoon salt
1 cup finely chopped pecans

Mix powdered sugar, margarine and vanilla. Stir in flour and salt. (If dough seems dry, mix in 3 to 4 teaspoons milk.) Shape into roll, about 2 inches in diameter. Roll in pecans. Wrap and refrigerate at least 4 hours.

Heat oven to 400°. Cut roll into ⅛-inch slices. Place about 1 inch apart on ungreased cookie sheet. Bake until light brown, 8 to 10 minutes. Immediately remove from cookie sheet.   ABOUT 6 DOZEN.

*Do not use self-rising flour in this recipe.

Molasses-Ginger Slices

Pictured on page 80.

1½ cups sugar
1½ cups shortening
 ¾ cup molasses
 4 cups all-purpose flour*
 1 tablespoon plus 1 teaspoon
      ground ginger
 1 tablespoon ground cinnamon
 1 tablespoon ground cloves
1½ teaspoons baking soda
1½ teaspoons salt
1½ cups finely chopped almonds

Mix sugar, shortening and molasses. Stir in remaining ingredients. Divide into halves. Shape each half into roll, about 2 inches in diameter. Wrap and refrigerate at least 3 hours.

Heat oven to 350°. Cut rolls into ¼-inch slices. Place on ungreased cookie sheet. Bake until almost no indentation remains when touched, about 9 minutes. Cool 2 minutes; remove from cookie sheet.   ABOUT 7 DOZEN.

*If using self-rising flour, omit baking soda and salt.

Peanut-Honey Slices

 ⅔ cup peanut butter
 ½ cup sugar
 ½ cup honey or corn syrup
 3 tablespoons shortening
 2 tablespoons plus 1 teaspoon margarine or
      butter, softened
 1 egg
 2 cups all-purpose flour*
 1 teaspoon baking powder
 ½ teaspoon salt
 ¼ teaspoon baking soda
 ½ cup finely chopped peanuts

Mix peanut butter, sugar, honey, shortening, margarine and egg. Stir in remaining ingredients. Shape into strip, about 10x2½x1½ inches. Wrap and refrigerate at least 8 hours.

Heat oven to 400°. Cut strip into ⅛-inch slices. Place on ungreased cookie sheet. Bake until light brown, 6 to 7 minutes.   ABOUT 4½ DOZEN.

*If using self-rising flour, omit baking powder and salt.

Cinnamon-Nut Slices

 1 cup packed brown sugar
 ¼ cup margarine or butter, softened
 ¼ cup shortening
 2 cups all-purpose flour*
 ¼ cup water
 1 teaspoon baking soda
 ½ teaspoon salt
 ½ teaspoon ground cinnamon
 ½ cup finely chopped nuts

Mix brown sugar, margarine and shortening. Stir in remaining ingredients. Shape into roll, about 2½ inches in diameter. Wrap and refrigerate at least 8 hours.

Heat oven to 400°. Cut roll into ⅛-inch slices. Place on ungreased cookie sheet. Bake until almost no indentation remains when touched, 6 to 7 minutes.   ABOUT 4 DOZEN.

*If using self-rising flour, omit baking soda and salt.

Nut-Molasses Slices

 1 cup all-purpose flour*
 ½ cup margarine or butter, softened
 ¼ cup powdered sugar
 2 tablespoons molasses
 ½ teaspoon vanilla
 ¼ teaspoon baking soda
 1 cup powdered sugar
 ⅓ cup margarine or butter, softened
 1 cup finely chopped nuts

Mix flour, ½ cup margarine, ¼ cup powdered sugar, the molasses, vanilla and baking soda. Divide into halves. Shape each half into roll, about 6 inches long. Wrap and refrigerate at least 4 hours.

Mix 1 cup powdered sugar, ⅓ cup margarine and the nuts. Divide into halves. Shape each half into roll, about 6 inches long. Wrap and refrigerate at least 4 hours. (Store doughs no longer than 6 weeks.)

Cut rolls into ¼-inch slices. Place molasses slices about 1 inch apart on ungreased cookie sheet; top each with nut-filled slice. Bake until delicate brown, 10 to 12 minutes. Immediately remove from cookie sheet.   ABOUT 3½ DOZEN.

*If using self-rising flour, omit baking soda.

Oatmeal-Coconut Slices

    1   cup granulated sugar
    1   cup packed brown sugar
    ½   cup margarine or butter, softened
    ½   cup shortening
    2   eggs
    1   teaspoon vanilla
    2½ cups all-purpose flour*
    1   teaspoon baking soda
    1   teaspoon salt
    1   cup oats
    1   cup flaked coconut

Mix sugars, margarine, shortening, eggs and vanilla. Stir in remaining ingredients. Divide into halves. Shape each half into roll, about 2 inches in diameter. Wrap and refrigerate at least 8 hours.

Heat oven to 400°. Cut rolls into ¼-inch slices. Place on ungreased cookie sheet. Bake until light brown, 8 to 9 minutes.   ABOUT 5 DOZEN.

*If using self-rising flour, omit baking soda and salt.

Oatmeal-Coconut Drops: Heat oven to 400°. Decrease flour to 1¾ cups. Drop dough by rounded teaspoonfuls about 2 inches apart onto ungreased cookie sheet.

Cereal Cookie Slices

    ½   cup sugar
    ½   cup margarine or butter, softened
    1   egg
    ½   teaspoon vanilla
    1½ cups all-purpose flour
    ½   teaspoon salt
    2   cups toasted oat cereal

Mix sugar, margarine, egg and vanilla. Stir in flour and salt. Mix in cereal. Divide into halves. Shape each half into roll, about 1½ inches in diameter. Wrap and refrigerate at least 4 hours.

Heat oven to 400°. Cut rolls into ¼-inch slices. Place about 1 inch apart on ungreased cookie sheet. Bake until light brown, 8 to 10 minutes. Immediately remove from cookie sheet.   ABOUT 6 DOZEN.

Spritz

    1   cup margarine or butter, softened
    ½   cup sugar
    2¼ cups all-purpose flour*
    1   teaspoon almond extract or vanilla
    ½   teaspoon salt
    1   egg

Heat oven to 400°. Mix margarine and sugar. Stir in remaining ingredients. Fill cookie press with dough; form desired shapes on ungreased cookie sheet. Bake until set but not brown, 6 to 9 minutes.   ABOUT 5 DOZEN.

*Do not use self-rising flour in this recipe.

Bow Tie Cookies: Stir 2 ounces melted unsweetened chocolate (cool) into margarine mixture. Using star plate on cookie press, form 2½-inch bow ties on ungreased cookie sheet. Place cinnamon candy in center. Bake 9 to 10 minutes.   ABOUT 3 DOZEN.

Chocolate Spritz: Stir 2 ounces melted unsweetened chocolate (cool) into margarine mixture.

Christmas-decorated Spritz: Before baking, top cookies with currants, raisins, candies, nuts or slices of candied fruits or candied fruit peels arranged in colorful and attractive patterns. Or after baking, decorate with colored sugars, nonpareils, red cinnamon candies and finely chopped nuts. Use drop of corn syrup to hold decorations on cookies.

Cigar Cookies: Stir 2 ounces melted unsweetened chocolate (cool) into margarine mixture. Using star plate on cookie press, form long strips of dough on ungreased cookie sheet. Cut into 3-inch lengths. Bake about 7 minutes. Dip 1 end of each cookie into Glaze (page 76), then dip into red sugar.   ABOUT 8 DOZEN.

Holiday Spritz

Pictured on page 67.

Heat oven to 400°. Prepare dough as directed for Spritz (page 89) except—substitute rum flavoring for the almond extract. Tint parts of dough with different food colors. After baking, glaze cooled cookies with Butter Rum Glaze (below) if desired.   ABOUT 5 DOZEN.

BUTTER RUM GLAZE

Heat ¼ cup margarine or butter over low heat until melted; remove from heat. Stir in 1 cup powdered sugar and 1 teaspoon rum flavoring. Beat in 1 to 2 tablespoons hot water until of desired consistency. Tint with different food colors to match cookies if desired.

Antoinettes

Heat oven to 400°. Prepare dough as directed for Spritz (page 89). Fill cookie press with dough. Using wide fluted plate on cookie press, form long strips of dough on ungreased cookie sheet. Cut into 2-inch lengths. Bake until set but not brown, 6 to 9 minutes. Immediately remove from cookie sheet. Just before serving, spread flat side of half of the cookies with raspberry preserves. Top with remaining cookies. Frost tops with Chocolate Frosting (below).   ABOUT 4 DOZEN.

CHOCOLATE FROSTING

Heat 2 tablespoons shortening and 1 square (1 ounce) unsweetened chocolate over low heat until melted; remove from heat. Stir in 1 cup powdered sugar and 2 tablespoons boiling water. Beat in few drops hot water, if necessary, until smooth and of spreading consistency.

Orange Crisps

    ½ cup granulated sugar
    ½ cup packed brown sugar
    ½ cup margarine or butter, softened
    ½ cup shortening
  2½ cups all-purpose flour*
    1 egg
    2 teaspoons grated orange peel
    1 tablespoon orange juice
    ¼ teaspoon baking soda
    ¼ teaspoon salt

Heat oven to 375°. Mix sugars, margarine and shortening. Stir in remaining ingredients. (If dough is too stiff, add egg yolk. If dough is not stiff enough, add small amounts of flour.) Fill cookie press with dough; form desired shapes on ungreased cookie sheet. Bake until light brown, 8 to 10 minutes.   ABOUT 6 DOZEN.

*If using self-rising flour, omit baking soda and salt.

Lemon Crisps: Substitute lemon peel and juice for the orange peel and juice.

Lemon-Cheese Cookies

    1 cup sugar
    1 cup margarine or butter, softened
    1 package (3 ounces) cream cheese,
         softened
    1 egg
    1 teaspoon grated lemon peel
    1 tablespoon lemon juice
  2½ cups all-purpose flour*
    1 teaspoon baking powder

Mix sugar, margarine, cream cheese, egg, lemon peel and lemon juice. Stir in flour and baking powder. Cover and refrigerate at least 30 minutes.

Heat oven to 375°. Fill cookie press with dough; form desired shapes on ungreased cookie sheet. Bake until light brown, 8 to 9 minutes. ABOUT 4 DOZEN.

*If using self-rising flour, omit baking powder.

Chocolate-Cheese Cookies: Omit lemon peel and lemon juice. Stir 2 ounces melted unsweetened chocolate (cool) into margarine mixture.

Cheese Cookie Wreaths

½ cup margarine or butter, softened
½ package (3-ounce size) cream cheese,
    softened
¼ cup sugar
½ teaspoon vanilla
1 cup all-purpose flour

Heat oven to 375°. Mix margarine and cream cheese. Stir in sugar. Beat in vanilla. Stir in flour gradually. Fill cookie press with dough. Using star plate, form wreath-shaped cookies on un-greased cookie sheet; gently push ends together. Bake until set but not brown, 8 to 10 minutes. Immediately remove from cookie sheet.   ABOUT 2 DOZEN.

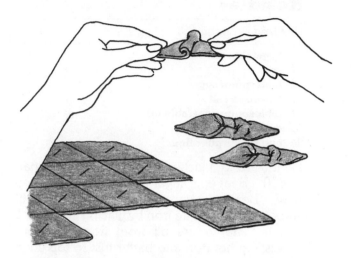

Viennese Shortbread

1 cup margarine or butter, softened
½ cup powdered sugar
½ teaspoon vanilla
2 cups all-purpose flour*
¼ teaspoon baking powder
    Mocha Filling (below)

Heat oven to 375°. Mix margarine, powdered sugar and vanilla. Stir in flour and baking powder. Fill cookie press with dough. Using medium star plate on cookie press, form 3-inch strips of dough on ungreased cookie sheet. Bake until edges are light brown, 7 to 9 minutes; cool. Put cookies together in pairs with Mocha Filling. For fancier cookies, dip edges in melted sweet chocolate.   ABOUT 20.

*If using self-rising flour, omit baking powder.

MOCHA FILLING
Mix 1 teaspoon powdered instant coffee and 1 teaspoon boiling water until coffee is dissolved. Mix in ⅔ cup powdered sugar and 2 tablespoons margarine or butter, softened. Stir in few drops water if necessary.

Crisp Fried Cookies

Also called *Fattigmann,* or Poor Man's Treat, in Norway these holiday cookies are prepared as long as a month ahead and stored in an airtight container.

10 egg yolks
⅓ cup powdered sugar
½ cup whipping cream
1 tablespoon cognac or other brandy
1 teaspoon ground cardamom
½ teaspoon grated lemon peel
2 to 2½ cups all-purpose flour*
    Vegetable oil
    Powdered sugar

Beat egg yolks and ⅓ cup powdered sugar until very thick and lemon colored, about 10 minutes. Stir in cream, cognac, cardamom and lemon peel. Mix in enough flour to make stiff dough. Cover and refrigerate at least 3 hours.

Heat oil (2 inches) in small deep saucepan to 375°. Divide dough into halves. Roll each half ¹⁄₁₆ to ⅛ inch thick on well-floured board. Cut dough into 4x2-inch diamonds with pastry wheel or knife. Make 1-inch crosswise slit in center of each; draw long point of diamond through slit and curl back in opposite direction. Fry until delicate brown, about 15 seconds on each side; drain on paper towels. Store in airtight container. Just before serving, sprinkle with powdered sugar.   ABOUT 4 DOZEN.

*Self-rising flour can be used in this recipe.

Rosettes

Pictured on page 29.

Vegetable oil
1 **egg**
1 **tablespoon sugar**
½ **teaspoon salt**
1 **tablespoon vegetable oil**
½ **cup water or milk**
½ **cup all-purpose flour** *

Heat oil (2 to 3 inches) in small deep saucepan to 400°. Beat egg, sugar and salt in small deep bowl. Beat in remaining ingredients until smooth. Heat rosette iron by placing in hot oil 1 minute. Tap excess oil from iron on paper towels; dip hot iron into batter just to top edge (don't go over top). Fry until golden brown, about 30 seconds. Immediately remove rosette; invert on paper towel to cool. (If rosette is not crisp, batter is too thick—stir in a small amount of water or milk.)

Heat iron in hot oil and tap on paper towels before making each rosette. (If iron is not hot enough, batter will not stick.) Just before serving, sprinkle with powdered sugar if desired. ABOUT 1½ DOZEN.

*If using self-rising flour, omit salt.

Krumkake

These Scandinavian delicacies are baked on a special iron and traditionally rolled around a wooden clothespin.

4 **eggs**
1 **cup sugar**
½ **cup margarine or butter, melted**
5 **tablespoons whipping cream**
1 **teaspoon vanilla**
¾ **cup all-purpose flour** *
2 **teaspoons cornstarch**

Heat ungreased *krumkake* iron over medium-high heat on smallest surface unit of electric or gas range. Beat all ingredients until smooth.

Test iron with few drops water; if they skitter around, iron is correct temperature. Drop ½ tablespoon batter on iron; close gently. Bake until light golden brown, about 15 seconds on each side. Keep iron over heat at all times. Remove cookie with knife. Immediately roll around wooden roller. (An old-fashioned clothespin works well.) ABOUT 6 DOZEN.

*Self-rising flour can be used in this recipe.

Index